PLAYS WELL WITH OTHERS

PLAYS WELL WITH OTHERS

UNSUNG HEROES OF THE ORCHESTRA
ACCORDING TO A HOLLYWOOD SESSION VIOLINIST
AND OTHER MUSICAL OFFERINGS

CONSTANCE MEYER

ISBN: 979-8-9953842-1-2 (Hardcover)
ISBN: 979-8-9953842-0-5 (Paperback)
ISBN: 979-8-9953842-2-9 (eBook)
ISBN: 979-8-9953842-3-6(Audiobook)

Book Cover and Interior Design by Theo Orion

IMAGE CREDITS

Cover images: *Yamaha Bass Tuba YFB-822* and *Yamaha Saxophone YAS-62* – Wikimedia Commons, CC BY-SA 4.0.

Interior images: *Film Scoring at BSO* – CC BY-SA 4.0; *Army Band, Verdun, France* and *"Seeing "Napoleon" - 1981" by Alan Light*, CC BY 2.0; *Swan Lake Panorama* – CC BY-SA 3.0.

Additional public domain or licensed images used in cover and interior are from The Metropolitan Museum of Art Open Access Collection, Smithsonian National Museum of African American History and Culture, Wikimedia Commons, Pexels, Shutterstock, and Rawpixel.

Some images were modified for layout, color, or stylistic consistency.

I dedicate this book to my siblings Deborah, Juliette and Nicholas Meyer, my daughters, Natasha and Tatiana Spottiswoode who all supported this project, but especially to my husband, James Spottiswoode, who believed in me long before I did.

CONTENTS

INTRODUCTION 1

PRELUDE 3

THE TUBA, A.K.A. THE BASS OF THE BRASS 7

PERCUSSION: PRECISION STRIKE FORCE 15

THE ENGLISH HORN: A MOURNFUL CRY OF 'AHHH' 23

VIOLAS: THEY'RE HARDLY SECOND STRING 31

THINK SAX AND YOU PROBABLY
WON'T THINK SYMPHONY 39

BASSOON: SYMPHONIC SPINE 47

DOUBLE BASS: ALWAYS THE HEAVY 55

THE HARP: HEAVEN FOR A PLUCKY FEW 65

ACCORDION: HOLDS A LOFTY PLACE 73

SECOND VIOLINISTS: FIRST-CLASS MUSICIANS 81

OTHER MUSICAL MUSINGS

THE MOM-CENTRIC METHOD......................................**91**

IRMA NEUMANN:

FIDDLING HER WAY THROUGH HISTORY **101**

BEYOND THE BRASS BANDS............................**107**

PIANO TECHNICIANS:

PULLING STRINGS TO GET IT RIGHT.....................**117**

CAPTURING A SOUND THAT RINGS TRUE **125**

AUER TO HEIFETZ **133**

SOVIET CONDUCTOR SURPASSES TRANSLATION **141**

VIVALDI IN A TIME OF WAR **147**

HOW I LEARNED TO LOVE OPERA **155**

PLAYING IN THE 'NAPOLEON' ORCHESTRA:

THE VIEW FROM THE VIOLIN SECTION.....................**159**

NOW YOU'RE HOT, NOW YOU'RE NOT.......................**165**

TEMP TRACK **179**

CODA...**189**

ACKNOWLEDGEMENTS **193**

INTRODUCTION

My sister Constance and I grew up in a family of musicians. One grandfather was a violinist in the Boston Symphony, a grandmother worshipped Wagner, an aunt was a triple threat, singer, violinist and orchestra conductor, my mother was a concert pianist and my father a gifted amateur pianist as well.

Following the family tradition, Constance became a violinist. And a violin teacher.

But there was another tradition in our family: writing. One aunt was a historian, our father the author of two biographies, and me, bringing up the rear, cranking out Sherlock Holmes and Star Trek movies.

In Constance, these two professions were united. A gifted musician and prose stylist, it was her happy idea to write about instruments in the symphony orchestra and the men and women who play them. Many folks are intimidated by what we call "classical music". This book will help them make sense of its components. Audiences experience the orchestra–that most miraculous of human achievements–in the aggregate; the contributions and tribulations of those who play in them are often ignored, overlooked or otherwise taken for granted.

Constance's book seeks to rectify this, focusing attention on the men, women and instruments that make the symphony orchestra the wonder that it is. In a sense, the book you hold in your hands is the verbal equivalent of Benjamin Britten's masterpiece, *The Young Person's Guide to the Orchestra*, but where Britten's ingenious music showcases each instrument, my sister's book adds fascinating details about the people who play them. Many of these mini-biographies originally appeared in the Calendar section of the Los Angeles Times and for years I have urged her to combine them into one volume where everyone can learn fun stuff about that fascinating and joyful contraption, the symphony orchestra.

I'm glad she finally got around to doing it.

NICHOLAS MEYER
Los Angeles, 2025

PRELUDE

I grew up in a musical family in 1950s New York City. My mother emigrated to the U.S. with her Russian parents when her violinist father joined the Boston Symphony. She would become a concert pianist. Her sister and one of my cousins were both conductors. Even my father, who in his day job was a psychiatrist, was a wonderful pianist. Growing up in this environment I couldn't help but absorb it. I began studying the violin when I was 5 and played in my first orchestra a few years later in the preparatory division of the Juilliard School.

I moved to Los Angeles in 1971 and began doing orchestra gigs and then studio work soon after. I played with wonderful musicians on great films. *Ghostbusters*, *Matilda*, *Body Heat*, some *Star Treks* to name just a few. I worked with Lalo Schifrin, Elmer Bernstein, John Barry, James Horner, and many more wonderful composers. Music was my livelihood, but I was passionate about writing, and did so on the QT.

In the summer of 2003, I received a phone call from Craig Fisher, the new Deputy Editor of the Los Angeles Times Sunday Calendar. Formerly at the Herald Examiner, the rival paper, Craig recalled reading some of my articles and asked if I would write for the Sunday Calendar. I accepted immediately, without thinking it through.

"What do you want to write about?" he asked me. Having had no time to think about this I blurted out:

"Why do we know about Soccer Moms and Stage Mothers but no one knows what a Suzuki Mom is?" I explained to him what they were and he said: "Go write it."

And so began my affiliation with the LA Times. Craig was an exceptionally generous mentor, who always improved my writing with his edits. I was free to write about anything musical so long as it wasn't about Disney Hall (which had just opened) or in the first person.

I decided to write a series about the unsung heroes of the orchestra, the musicians who slave away at their instruments but are in the shadows of the symphony, unlike the violins or trumpets or other extrovert instruments. While I never specifically titled the series, in my head it was "A Middle-Aged Person's Guide to the Lesser-Known Instruments of the Orchestra." I loved hearing from musicians why they were drawn to their instrument, what experiences were memorable.

After a few of these articles came out the Times asked me to write about something musically adjacent as well. Hence the other musical offerings.

THE TUBA, A.K.A. THE BASS OF THE BRASS

Tuba players may be the Rodney Dangerfields of the orchestra, but the instrument has come a long way since its creation in the 1830s
January 18, 2004

CHILDREN of the '50s and '60s may remember *Tubby the Tuba* — the story, set to music, of a very shy brass instrument in a symphony orchestra. All Tubby wants is a solo. If his saga rings a bell, however, it's probably because of the narrator of the 1947 recording, Danny Kaye, and not the tuba player, Los Angeles musician George Bouie, who doesn't even get a credit on the CD version.

That lack of respect has long plagued the tuba, a Johnny-come-lately to the modern orchestra. While the violin was perfected more than 300 years ago, the tuba didn't exist until the 1830s, when early versions began to evolve from the German ophicleide, a woodwind-like brass instrument that seems to have deeply under-whelmed composers.

Hector Berlioz wrote extensively about his dislike for the ophi-cleide, and he was the first composer to write specifically for the modern tuba. Indeed, a three-week series of concerts the Los Angeles Philharmonic began Thursday to mark his bicentenary means an unusually large amount of playing for the orchestra's tuba player, 46-year-old Norman Pearson.

After Berlioz, Wagner used so-called Wagner tubas in the *Ring* cycle, Stravinsky chose the tuba to accompany the Dancing Bear in the 1910 ballet *Petrushka*, and Ravel highlighted it in his 1922 orchestration of Mussorgsky's *Pictures at an Exhibition*. Where the double bass is the bass voice of the string family, the tuba, in all its varieties, became the bass voice of the brass.

Still, there's George Kleinsinger's *Tubby the Tuba*. Unlike Prokofiev's score for the narrated tale *Peter and the Wolf*, it is not great music, but it resonates deeply with tuba players. Jim Self, one of the busiest in L.A., says: "I've lived it. Most tuba players have."

So why does anyone take up such an enormous, heavy and convoluted instrument, which can make a player look caught in the grip of a shiny boa constrictor? Tommy Johnson, 69, another prominent local tubist, was the youngest of five children and the only boy, and so, he recalls: "I definitely didn't want to play the piano or a stringed instrument." His father, a singer and choir director, suggested trumpet.

"Three years later," Johnson says, "I went to our band director and asked if I could join." The reply: " 'No, we have way too many trumpet players. But if you could play that thing back there' — he pointed to something in the dark corner in the back of the room, there's this dingy old-looking tuba — 'If you could play that, you could probably be in the band. Soon.' "

The modest Johnson says: "You just read the bass clef like a treble clef, add some flats and sharps, and it works. I was in the band the next week."

TUBIST ALSO A FLUBIST

Self, now 60, took up the guitar at age 9. But, he says, "guitar is not a school instrument. The band needed a tuba/sousaphone player, and I said I had some musical training. I got to play in marching bands of all kinds — volunteer firemen's, community, American Legion. I was a young kid who got to play with these older guys. The tuba was foisted on me, and I took it over."

Today, when not playing in one of the five area orchestras he belongs to or on a recording date, Self is probably working in the stunning two-story studio behind his home in Laurel Canyon. "Jim eats, sleeps and breathes tuba," says the Philharmonic's Pearson, who has studied with Self, so it's not surprising to find a tuba-shaped window in the main room amid surfaces glistening with brass instruments and memorabilia. Self has recorded several CDs, both classical and jazz. The latest, *My America*, even features an instrument he dreamed up: a tuba-sized fluegelhorn built for him by Robb Stewart of Arcadia. Self dubbed it the fluba.

For Self, it's essential to commission and write music for the tuba that shows off not only his own abilities but the instrument's versatility. "It can't be a comic instrument," he says. "It can't be a buffoon. It can't be *Tubby the Tuba*, getting out once a year in front of the orchestra."

However, he acknowledges, "the low brass are considered the jokesters of the orchestra. We have a lot of free time and cut up, make jokes and drive everybody crazy. We have a lot less to play than the violins — but if you miss a note, boy, everybody hears it."

Apart from the potential peril of a resounding clinker, tubists face a couple of major hurdles. For one, they must be "doublers," capable of playing more than just their own instrument. They have traditionally doubled on bass trombone, cimbasso and sousaphone, but because they played double bass parts for early recordings — on which the double bass proved inaudible — they are often expected to be proficient bass players as well.

More important, of the 90 or so musicians who make up a full symphony orchestra, there is only one tuba player. As Pearson puts it: "It can be 30 years before a job opens up." Arnold Jacobs, for instance, was 29 when he became the Chicago Symphony's tubist; he didn't retire until 45 years later. And the competition is so fierce that any opening attracts hundreds of applicants.

If there's a granddaddy to all these hopefuls, he's probably New York tubist Harvey Phillips, now 74. In "The Tuba Source Book," a nearly 2-inch-thick volume containing everything you'd ever want to know about the instrument, he has the longest bio. Beyond "being just a great tuba player," Pearson says, Phillips has been a "musical entrepreneur. He's taught a lot of young tuba players how to make a living playing music, how to create their own opportunities." It was Phillips who looked squarely at the quandary of tubists and organized them the way a military strategist would.

In the '50s, Phillips was a founding member of the New York Brass Quintet, which led many colleges that already had a string quartet in residence to add a brass quintet. He started and was the first president of TUBA — the Tubists Universal Brotherhood Assn., now called the International Tuba Euphonium Assn. He also commissioned hundreds of tuba pieces and encouraged other tubists, who did the same. The literature expanded dramatically. Two important works that resulted in the mid-'50s were Paul Hindemith's Tuba Sonata and Ralph Vaughan Williams' Tuba Concerto.

In addition, Phillips organized conferences, journals and TubaChristmas — annual concerts of carols and other holiday music held in more than 130 cities and countries. Self has produced

Los Angeles' TubaChristmas for 28 years. Last month, the event brought together nearly 300 tuba/euphonium players and a sing-along audience of almost 2,000. On Dec. 21, there was even a TubaChristmas in Tikrit, Iraq.

MOVIE SPOTLIGHT

There's no doubt the tuba has come a long way in 160 years. According to Johnson, "the instrument really took on a different role, not just a supporting role but also a solo role." In the movie *Jaws*, it represented the shark the first time the deadly creature swam into view. Composer John Williams explained to Johnson that he wanted "something that would sound more menacing than the French horn but would have a nice lyrical quality." In another Williams score, *Close Encounters of the Third Kind*, the voice of the mother ship was played by Self.

Unfortunately, Self will be absent from the huge tuba call for the *Berlioz Requiem* when the Philharmonic tackles that masterpiece in June (the composer's original orchestration called for six or seven tubas out of 500 musicians) because he'll be performing Vaughan Williams' Tuba Concerto with the Pacific Symphony.

Certainly, L.A.-born Roger Bobo, who was with the Philharmonic from 1964 to 1989, proved that the tuba can be a virtuoso instrument. In 1961, Bobo, now 65, played the first solo tuba recital at Carnegie Recital Hall. Later, he and Johnson performed the first movement of Bach's fleet-footed Concerto for Two Violins with the Philharmonic under Zubin Mehta.

Yet despite its improved status, the tuba has not entirely lost its talent to amuse. A few years ago, Johnson says, "I got this call: 'Can you play *Hava Nagila* on the tuba?'" The occasion, it turned out, was a surprise party for a woman engaged to be married, who frequently joked that she mustn't forget her ketubah, or Jewish wedding contract. Her friends, though, kept reminding her, "Don't forget to bring the tuba." "So I'm sitting in the middle of all these people and nobody asks, 'What are you doing here?'The door opens and I start to play and she says, 'The tuba!'"

PERCUSSION: PRECISION STRIKE FORCE

New music and technology have them taking up a whole new world of noise toys, but L.A. pros agree that one thing hasn't changed: Accuracy is key

May 23, 2004

THE percussion section stands at the back of the orchestra, facing the conductor, gladiators poised for battle. These warriors are armed with their bare hands, mallets, sticks and scores of other utensils that can tap, hit, scrape, shake, pound, bow — you name it — to get a response from literally thousands of instruments. Kiddie percussion kits may make what they do look like child's play, but it requires the precision of a marksman.

No wonder the assassin in Alfred Hitchcock's *The Man Who Knew Too Much*, charged with firing a deadly shot in a concert hall just as a cymbal crashes, receives a brief course in musical timing.

Indeed, the late George Plimpton, who famously chronicled

making his Walter Mitty-style dreams come true, described playing triangle with the New York Philharmonic as far more difficult than playing quarterback with the Detroit Lions. "I found myself not being able to fall asleep nights," he wrote. "The mental anguish is multiplied by the fear of coming in on the wrong note, that you might damage the entire performance."

Since the Stone Age, percussion instruments have played a major role in every culture — in communication, ceremonies, the military. But unlike the other sections of the orchestra, which have remained relatively unchanged for hundreds of years, the percussion section is constantly growing. In the Baroque period, it consisted basically of timpani: two kettledrums with fixed pitches. Over time, it came to include instruments that were both pitched, or set to a specific tone, and nonpitched. By now, just about anything's fair game. The most famous number in Verdi's *Il Trovatore*, which begins a nine-performance run at Los Angeles Opera on Thursday, is the Anvil Chorus. Verdi hoped for an anvil in the pit; L.A. Opera substitutes four lengths of pipe.

Often, a passion for percussion seizes a player in childhood. Emil Richards was 6 when he made such a fuss at a music store while his older brother was getting an accordion that his father shouted, "What do you want?!" Emil "just pointed. I didn't care.... It was a xylophone."

Despite the capriciousness of that choice, Richards took to his new instrument immediately. Sixty-five years later, he is one of Los Angeles' foremost mallet players — specializing in instruments, like the xylophone and marimba, that produce melodies when struck — and is world-renowned for his skills on his huge collection of exotic percussion instruments. He has played on innumerable film scores and worked with Frank Sinatra, George Shearing, Ravi Shankar, Frank Zappa and the Beatles. And he learned early on the importance of accuracy in his trade.

By the time he was a 10th-grader in Connecticut, Richards was good enough to be recruited to appear with the Hartford Symphony under guest conductor Arthur Fiedler. Leroy Anderson's *Classical Jukebox* required the fledgling to hit a cowbell with a silver dollar. But because his eyes were glued to the conductor, he missed the bell, hit a French horn player, lost his grip on the coin and watched helplessly as it rolled down the risers and landed, after a lengthy spin, at Fiedler's feet. The conductor retrieved it, walked purposefully up the risers and said to the tuxedoed 16-year-old: "Shall we try it again?"

Now, when teaching, Richards stresses to his students the importance of peripheral vision.

A PATH FROM ROCK

Not every percussionist comes to orchestral work after years of study. Peter Limonick, 55, made the journey by way of rock 'n' roll. "I could play a good backbeat," he says. Limonick, a much-in-demand studio player, had studied piano and classical guitar and was accustomed to hearing his father, Marvin, a professional violinist, practice and play chamber music with friends. But it was a recording of Bartok's *Music for Strings, Percussion and Celesta* that "locked me up as a potential player." Limonick and his father would "break out Mozart or early Beethoven string quartets. I'd play my part on xylophone or marimba. Any violinist who would play string quartets with a xylophone player is either crazy or he's got a lot of love."

In 1970, Limonick won an audition to "earn as you learn" in the percussion section of the Milwaukee Symphony. The first concert he participated in included Elgar's *Enigma Variations*. "I was playing cymbals," he remembers. "A part to be reckoned with. The basses come in on a low G and the floor is shaking. It was just so gorgeous I stopped counting and didn't know where I was. I was out of my league. Somehow I managed to catch myself, came in on my first entrance and was off and running.

"If you've never sat in the percussion section, you wouldn't know that acoustically, it is not the ideal spot," he adds. "It's so loud. And there's lag time. The ultimate place would be principal oboe or flute. You've got full surround sound and you're close enough to the strings to lock in with them."

Tom Raney, 54, timpanist with the Los Angeles Chamber Orchestra, the Pasadena Symphony and the Hollywood Bowl Orchestra, took yet another career path. Raney, who also plays on studio dates, started out as a piano player, but competing with a drummer for a woman's attentions persuaded him to change course. He went on to study at USC with some of Los Angeles' finest in the percussion realm: Ken Watson, William Kraft and Earl Hatch.

"One of the great things about playing percussion," Raney says, "is that we probably have the best palette of any of the instruments of the orchestra. Between the variety of instruments, the materials used on those instruments, the range, the dynamic capability, we just have more fun than anybody. Boys with toys."

Actually, there are a number of women in today's percussion sections. Theresa Dimond, 45, was recently appointed principal percussionist with the Los Angeles Opera and is timpanist with the Pasadena Pops and the California Philharmonic. She also plays frequently with the Pasadena Symphony and the Los Angeles Master Chorale.

Although Dimond auditioned to enter USC as an undergraduate on piano, oboe and percussion, she was offered a full scholarship on percussion. And at 17, she recalls, she didn't "realize what the repercussions of that decision" would be: "You're going to have to buy 18 timpani, marimba and other instruments by the time you're done, as well as move all your equipment around. I weighed about 100 pounds."

Dimond has one carpet bag for timpani sticks, another for percussion sticks and mallets and a third for bass drum and gong beaters. "Mallets are like shoes. You can never have enough," she says. But hauling around her delicate, easily crushed mallets for the cimbalon — a sort of oversized dulcimer — has become harder since 9/11. "It's just a PVC piping tube. But apparently it looks like a pipe bomb."

Sitting at her dining room table — a 2-inch-thick sheet of glass atop two enormous American-made taiko drums — Dimond confides that being principal percussionist with Los Angeles Opera can be "more of a treasure hunt than worrying about playing a tough 16th note lick." It is her responsibility to rent the pitched gongs for *Madame Butterfly* and arrange for the anvil-sounding pipes for *Il Trovatore*.

Dimond also says she's had to learn how to bide her time gracefully. "I had 11 notes in *Flying Dutchman*," she explains. "Over the course of three hours. Three notes in the first act and eight in the last. Patience is a virtue when you're a percussionist. We don't have melodies often. We add color, chime midnight, play thunder, crank a canvas-covered barrel for wind."

Raney, for his part, recalls "years ago doing *Die Meistersinger*. You play the overture and I think the first scene and then it says an hour and 29 minutes' rest. You left the pit, went next door to the Curtain Call restaurant, had dinner, came back. And while you were there, since *Die Meistersinger* is 4 1/2 to five hours long, so are half of the singers — in costume."

In more contemporary music, by contrast, the challenges to percussionists have snowballed. "In the 20th century, the range of the drums increased because the mechanism for tuning them became easier," Raney says. "Today, some studio parts are almost equal to the bass parts, so we're trying to figure out, if you only have six drums but you have to play 12 different pitches during the cue, where and when to change, and what pitch to put where. I've often said I sold my soul to the devil so I can play in tune. I will use my ears, gauges, electronic tuners, any trick I can to get a drum in tune. You can tell when your drums are in tune because they open up. They sing."

MORE THINGS TO HIT

Beyond that, the number of instruments that percussionists may be expected to be proficient on is constantly rising. Larry Bunker, 75, is perhaps the most beloved member of the local percussion community. He's played live or on record with a host of jazz greats, including Billie Holiday, Gerry Mulligan and Bill Evans. Bunker says he was first smitten with percussion at age 4. His older brother helped him collect "pots, pans, cardboard boxes, stuff you could find in the trash" to play on, but by 1953 he was working as a sit-down drummer, vibraphonist and piano player in jazz clubs. Yet the self-taught Bunker recalls an audition that year he says was typical of the percussionist's lot: Cabaret singer Bobby Short asked if he could play congas; when he said no, Short responded, "Well, if you want the job, go get a drum, get it together, 'cause I have to have it — or I have to get somebody else."

Still, "the demands on the players on percussion at that time were nothing like what they are now," Bunker says. "Nobody dared write the kind of music they do today. If I were to show up now as ill-equipped as I was then, it never would've happened."

Bunker did learn the congas. So did Michael Fisher, who was a

15-year-old in Denver 30 years ago, playing lead guitar and singing with a rock band, when he was called upon to pound the elongated drums. He became so fascinated that he eventually moved to Los Angeles to pursue a career in world/ethnic percussion. Today he plays everything from the bodhran, an Irish frame drum, to udu drums — fired Nigerian clay pots.

"When I started, it was very difficult to find instruments," he says. "You usually had to go to that country. Or maybe there was one guy here in town who had a couple of drums, and there'd be word of mouth. I like when I get into an instrument. I'll just stick with that instrument for a while. I'll try to search out who's the best player in the real ethnic world, in town. Take the Egyptian tambourine, the riq. There's a guy in Vegas who's just fantastic on it. I would get lessons when he'd come to town. For several years I was just pretty much working on tabla."

Although many musicians now do electronic percussion, Fisher was an early player in that field as well. Among the more esoteric sounds he has "sampled" is a "cowling from a 747 engine — rolling marbles in it."

"For the last few years, there's been more hand percussion and groove-type playing, getting a part where there's just slashes," he says. "There's not much written. They ask you to come up with ideas and work with you to find which ideas work best for the piece.

"There's always something else to learn. Currently I'm studying with Persian percussionist Houman Pourmehdi, learning to play the instruments called dayre and daf as well as learning to apply tombak finger techniques applied to the Spanish or Peruvian cajon. Our middle names are maintenance."

In fact, asked whether he ever gets bored, Tom Raney probably speaks for most working percussionists: "Are you kidding? I get to do this for a living!"

THE ENGLISH HORN: A MOURNFUL CRY OF 'AHHH'

The curvy instrument requires its player to pack a lot of wind — the better to produce those sad sounds. And watch out for the razor blades
May 23, 2004

DECADES ago, Ripley's Believe It or Not clued readers in about the English horn. The instrument, it declared, is "neither English nor a horn."

In fact, there's little agreement about where the name of this double-reed woodwind, a member of the oboe family, came from — only consensus that it's a misnomer.

Good luck if you query an Englishman about it. Show him a picture and he might well correct you: "Oh, you mean the cor anglais."

But as Carolyn Hove, the English horn player with the Los Angeles Philharmonic, says with a laugh: "It wouldn't take much for cor anglé" — a possible reflection in French that the instrument was originally angled to make playing it on horseback easier — "to become cor anglais. It's probably one of those evolution things, where one thing led to another and it's just one giant misunderstanding."

Certainly many people recognize the oboe, straight and black with its silver keys, when it plays an A so the members of the orchestra can tune their instruments. Far fewer listeners can distinguish its curvy cousin. To cognoscenti, though, the English horn's sound — its urgent plangency — is bolder, deeper, richer.

"A brass player uses a mouthpiece," Hove says, "then buzzes his lips. With the double-reed instruments, it's the two reeds vibrating against each other between the lips and the airstream that make the tone."

Oboist and English hornist Kim Gilad, a member of the Los Angeles Chamber Orchestra and a busy freelancer, notes that in film scores, the English horn is "usually used in sad, mysterious or poignant scenes, much the way the sax is used in sexy ones."

To Earle Dumler, who plays oboe and English horn with Los Angeles Opera, the sound is "mournful." Dumler remembers the late actor-producer Michael Landon's words to him at a Christmas party for TV's *Little House on the Prairie*, on which he played for 11 years: "Earle, as long as they're crying and dying, you'll be working."

CURVE MAKES A DIFFERENCE

At first glance, the English horn resembles an overgrown oboe. But it has two things an oboe doesn't: First there's the bell shape at the bottom, which looks, if you've spent any time around school science labs, like the bulge in a snake that has recently devoured a mouse. Second is the reed holder — the bocal (rhymes with "vocal"). Hove describes it as a "little angled metal tube, smaller at the top, a little larger as it goes down. It's got a curve to it and some cork around the outside of the bottom, which goes into the reed well."

"This curve is one of the things that changes the sound," she explains, "as opposed to the oboe, which is a straight shot.

The English horn's greater heft, it turns out, is part of its appeal to many players: Specialists refer to the comfort of its size. Whereas the soprano-voiced oboe is petite, its tenor-voiced relative, pitched five notes lower, is a better fit in certain musicians' hands.

Conversely, not all oboists learn to play the English horn because, as Gilad notes, "it's quite a bit heavier, and they find it uncomfortable. Some people get tendinitis in their arms, so they specialize on oboe and audition for those jobs." And some English horn specialists, like Stuart Horn, feel "constricted" playing the oboe. Although the busy Horn won a Grammy this year on oboe with Southwest Chamber Music in the small ensemble performance category, "with the English horn," he says, "I feel I can sing."

Still, many orchestras don't have an English horn chair; the second oboist simply "doubles" on the instrument. Dumler, for example, hails from a small town in Kansas where, he says, "two things were big in the school system — basketball and music." At the beginning of sixth grade, he recalls, he was asked what instrument he wanted to learn. His confident reply: "Oboe." Thus he was perplexed when the teacher "came out with a little case. I had it confused in my mind with the bassoon. But I was much too proud to admit my error, so I stuck with it.

"I was always attracted to strange, obscure instruments," he adds, but "the high school didn't even own an English horn because there was no one who could play it."

He finally got his hands on one when he went to study at the New England Conservatory of Music in Boston, where he also found that "oboe players could be very arrogant: 'Play the English horn? Certainly not.' " The result? "They stayed home — and I worked."

Joan Elardo has held the English horn chair with the Long Beach Symphony since 1987, after a number of years playing oboe frequently with the Los Angeles Philharmonic. And becoming known for her English horn playing, she acknowledges, produced mixed feelings: "I just kept getting called for English horn, and it made my oboe persona envious. In my head, I was always a principal oboe player, and the English horn was like a poor relation. You played English horn because you weren't good enough to play first oboe, right?"

More so than the oboe, though, playing the English horn takes unusual stamina. Gilad likens it to "blowing up one of those hard balloons that you do for your kids. Try doing that for two hours. It's a very physical instrument because you're blowing through a very tiny opening. There's a lot of back pressure. It's helpful if you run or swim or do something to keep your lungs strong."

Hove, whose mother was a violinist, notes that string players don't have "wind" issues. "They can play on for pages and pages. We can't do that. We have to breathe and give our embouchure a chance to recover. You have to let these muscles" — she touches her lips and the facial and jaw muscles used to blow into the instrument — "time to relax before you can go on."

But the slogan on one of Stuart Horn's T-shirts — "Got reed?" — pinpoints the biggest hassle for double-reed players. As Hove puts it: "We spend millions of hours at our reed desks."

Gilad explains: "Reeds are made out of bamboo, which has to be split, gouged, shaped and scraped so this little piece of cane can vibrate. And it needs to be wet to do that." Says Hove: "The cane starts out at around 4 inches long. Then we fold it over so it becomes half as long, tie it onto the tube, scrape and clip and so on. I know some players who can have a television on, or listen to music. I can't. I have to be completely focused on what I'm doing.

"We've all gotten cut," she adds. "We use single-edge razor blades and sharp knives. But you learn."

The reeds — which have a performing life comparable to that of toe shoes — need to be moist for an English hornist to play well, and these musicians' "space" onstage reveals a fair amount of additional paraphernalia not only to produce moisture but to then extract it from their instruments. To soak his reeds, Horn takes a thermos with "warmish water" that he places with other tools under his seat; some players use a 2-inch film canister. Most players also routinely run a delicate silk scarf, a "swab," through their instruments.

"We swab out the hot air that we're blowing in, which creates moisture, so the moisture doesn't crack the wood," Gilad says. Elardo stopped using her purple swab after it got stuck in her instrument once too often. These days, she "swabs out" with a turkey feather.

The price of a top-quality English horn is about $10,000. Hove says that "while it's cheap compared to a stringed instrument" — a Stradivarius can fetch millions — "we have to have more than one, and they wear out. Unlike stringed instruments that appreciate with the years, ours depreciate and get damaged with use, so you're constantly looking to replace instruments."

On the other hand, there are, by general agreement, only two important oboe and English horn makers. As with Coke and Pepsi, you're in one camp or the other. Dumler, Gilad and Horn play instruments made by Paul Laubin, a New Yorker whose father, Al, started the business. Elardo and Hove play Loree instruments, made in Paris. Horn considers himself "very lucky to have a Laubin

English horn, because he's closed his list, meaning it'll take him the rest of his life to fill the orders he now has. I have a new oboe coming from him in a couple of weeks, so he's still cranking those out. The waiting list for a rosewood oboe is about six years."

IT'S A WORKOUT

One of the difficulties of writing a concerto for English horn, Hove says, is "the issues of fatigue on your embouchure." All the same, Gilad remembers a stunning performance by Hove of Saint-Saëns' *The Swan*, originally written for cello: "That piece just keeps going and going. There's no place to rest, and you're just holding long notes most of the time. That's one of the big pieces for English horn. Ravel's Piano Concerto in G major is another." Hove will play in the Ravel on Tuesday, when the Philharmonic performs it at the Hollywood Bowl with soloist Orli Shaham.

Last year, Hove played in the premiere of the Concerto for English Horn and Orchestra by the Philharmonic's former timpanist and composer in residence, William Kraft; he also dedicated the piece to her. But although she has recorded two solo CDs, she observes that "you can't make a career of playing concerti with orchestras the way a percussionist like Evelyn Glennie can. There are solo pieces and a certain amount of concerti, but it's not a mainstream instrument." Within the context of the orchestra, "we get glorious solos, but then the English horn is also used as an inner voice, the way the French horns are used, or the viola."

Composers also have not written consistently for the instrument. Although in his choral music Bach wrote gorgeous solos for its predecessor, the oboe da caccia — as well as for the English horn — the latter was all but completely ignored throughout the Classical period. Only one of Haydn's 100-plus symphonies, *The*

Philosopher, calls for it.

"You didn't find it in Brahms, Beethoven, Mendelssohn or Schumann," Hove says. By contrast, Berlioz, who included a number of formerly marginalized instruments in his broadening of symphonic orchestration, "used the English horn on a regular basis. Debussy, Ravel, Stravinsky, Wagner and Richard Strauss wrote a lot for the English horn, as did many of the 20th century composers."

According to Dumler, "probably the biggest parts for English horn are in opera. Wagner used it a lot." *Tristan and Isolde* offers one example; Dumler has performed it a number of times with Los Angeles Opera. "There are about five offstage solos," he says. "The opening of the third act, the English horn is alone for 12 to 15 minutes. There's a shepherd onstage. You have a television monitor and your own conductor just to bring you in." Hove will be playing those passages with the Philharmonic during the coming season, when the entire opera will be performed over several concerts.

For Elardo, the tone of the English horn is "plaintive. So many of the solos are gut-wrenching, 'let it all hang out.' I guess I'm real good at that. I'm half Italian-Spanish and half Russian Jew. All my life, I always poured all my emotion into the instrument, and English horn just seems to accept it better. I can't say why. Part of it is the repertoire, part of it is the color, and part of it is that it's more flexible in a way that the oboe isn't."

Any hard feelings between the oboe and the English horn camps?

Elardo sighs. "That's the sad part. Oboe players work their butts off. They play everything, and the English horn player sits there all night, plays an eight-bar solo, and everybody just goes, 'Ahhhh.'"

VIOLAS: THEY'RE HARDLY SECOND STRING

They don't get much respect, as an entire genre of jokes proves. But try building a quartet without one
December 12, 2004

FEW violists are born. Most have the instrument thrust upon them. In fact, the viola — the overlooked stepchild of the orchestra's string section — is rarely studied as a first instrument at all. Until fairly recently, the road to mastering it invariably went through years of study on the violin, which is both smaller and pitched a fifth higher.

Today, some novices do start on the viola. High school orchestra conductors have been known to entice kids to take it up by noting that "it looks good on your college application." Why? Because fewer young people study it, and they're always in demand for orchestras and chamber music groups.

Yet despite usually being hidden behind the conductor, all but invisible to many concertgoers, violas and violists have long been the butt of jokes, of which there are untold thousands. And the instrument seems to inspire, if not outright derision, then indifference or just plain confusion.

Dan Neufeld, a busy L.A. studio violist, says: "Very often, you'll be introduced to somebody and you say, 'I play the viola,' and the next time they see you they'll say, 'How's the cello?' The mind says it's a stringed instrument and it's not the violin." Another frequent comment, he says, is "Gee, I go to the symphony all the time, and I've never seen a viola."

Years ago, Neufeld suffered a neck injury in an automobile accident. "I was going to an orthopedist and undergoing physical therapy," he recalls. "I said, 'Doc, you know I play the viola for a living? Much as I'd hate to lose the work, do you think maybe it would be a good idea for me to take a rest?' " The physician's response, he says, was: "No, I don't think playing the viola should be a problem." "So I did my couple of weeks of playing and my neck was getting worse, and I told him, 'You know, holding that viola under my chin is really killing my neck.' " The response then? "Oh! Is that how you play the viola?"

Neufeld admits that when he was younger, his own attitude toward the instrument was somewhat contemptuous, "programmed" by his violinist father, Erno, for 40 years the concertmaster at Universal Studios. Dan Neufeld was a violin major at UCLA when a professor in a chamber music class took a viola out of its case and said: "You will play the viola." "I was reluctant to even touch it!" he says. But "I have fairly long arms, and the violin always felt a little cramped. I played the first note of viola and said, 'My goodness, this is fun!' "

Pam Goldsmith, an adjunct professor of viola at USC and a past recipient of the "most valuable player" award from the National

Academy of Recording Arts & Sciences, tells a similar story. She was "just an ordinary kid in the third grade" when she began violin lessons in the Los Angeles public school system. At about age 15, while fraternizing with a violist during an orchestra break, she startled herself by saying, " 'Hey, let me try your viola.' I just played a few notes, and the heavens opened up and lightning struck. I knew this was my voice."

Now, Goldsmith says, she never misses an opportunity to educate the public. "I'll be standing in an elevator holding my viola case and people will say, 'What's that?' 'A viola. It's the alto member of the string family. It's larger than a violin. It has a much more beautiful, mellow tone,' and I keep right on talking till the elevator doors open."

So is there a violist personality? According to Goldsmith, "Yes. You don't want to be a star. You're never going to play the Wieniawski Concerto. You do it because you love it, because you enjoy understanding the structure of the music, not just the melody. When you're in the center, for example, playing a Brahms symphony, the music swirling all around you, it's the most incredible aural experience — thrilling."

Until he was in his mid-30s, Brian Dembow was a successful concert violinist. But he had long played viola as well, and he finally decided to take it up full time. Now he's the violist with the Angeles Quartet and a first-call freelancer. "I have to say my personality is much better suited to playing the viola," he says. "I don't need to be in the limelight. I'm happy being in a supportive role. I find it less stressful not being part of the energy that surrounds violinists and that they help create themselves."

Violists may also have less of a competitive streak than many musicians. Like Goldsmith, Roland Kato, principal violist with the Los Angeles Chamber Orchestra, began studying the violin in the L.A. school system. And in his junior high orchestra, he says, he won the seat of concertmaster. The trouble was, by doing so he dethroned its previous occupant.

"She had a stage mom and was very upset, crying, blubbering, 'My mother's going to kill me because I lost the chair.' I didn't understand what she was talking about, because my parents" — Japanese immigrants — "weren't pushy or manipulative. She challenged me a bit later for her seat. I said, 'Forget it, I don't care.' I just moved into the viola section." Kato then experienced a "seminal moment" that led him to make the move permanent: "I had put the violin on my bed and was getting things from the shelf above, and things fell on the violin. The thing that actually made the bridge go through the instrument was a Ouija board. I took it as a definite sign."

THE PHYSICAL CHALLENGE

Traditionally larger than a violin, the viola does require extra capability. Says Dembow: "You have to be accommodating physically to play the instrument. If violin is not the most natural instrument in the world, viola is even more so." When he first tried playing it as a teenager, "it felt really miserable — ungainly and uncomfortable."

At 6-foot-2, Kazi Pitelka certainly has the physical equipment for the task. The principal violist for Los Angeles Opera since 1991, she looks back fondly to 1974, when she went to audition for Lillian Fuchs, the 4-foot-9 grande dame violist and renowned teacher. Fuchs "whipped open the door, her eyes going all the way from my feet up to my head. 'Dearie, you were born to play the viola!' When I played the viola, she could walk under it. That's how tall I am and how small she was."

In addition to her opera work, Pitelka does studio dates, is principal violist for the Los Angeles Master Chorale and the Long Beach Symphony, and is a member of the chamber group Xtet, now in its 20th year. But opera, she says, is "exceptionally strenuous. It hurts. It takes stamina. It's very hard. Playing Richard Strauss' *Die Frau Ohne Schatten* is like playing Mahler's Fifth, taking an intermission, playing Mahler's Fifth, taking an intermission and doing it a third time. The sheer weight of a large viola can really be problematic and lead to overuse injury. Some people play on a small viola to try to protect themselves. But in truth, bigger violas sound better, so you want to find some way to get the volume and the string length without having too much weight."

As Goldsmith puts it, no matter your height, playing the viola is an "athletic event." And as Pitelka suggests, violists, in particular, are prey to repetitive stress syndrome, which can cause pain and inflammation in their wrists, elbows and shoulders. To understand why, Goldsmith says, "all you have to do is look at the viola part in a score. So often we are called upon to play a rhythmic figure over and over to accompany a melody."

Another part of the problem, Goldsmith explains, is "there is no standardization in the size of the viola. They basically come in small, medium and large. You have to find an instrument that fits your body. When I started out, there were very few women violists, and most of the men played large violas. I remember at an audition the conductor said to me, 'That's a small viola you're playing,' and I said, 'Yes,' and he said, 'I wouldn't let anyone in my section play a viola so small.'"

Times have changed, though. Most musicians hesitate to acknowledge any injury, lest it affect their job prospects. But increasingly, there's more experimentation with viola size and sound. "I think there's been a move now for people to just get comfortable," Goldsmith says — meaning that today's violists are not ashamed to play smaller instruments.

There are even some players who are courageous enough, or desperate enough, to buck tradition and use one of the ergonomically designed Pellegrina violas made by Oregonian David Rivinus. Though distasteful to purists because of their stretched yet shrunken appearance, these instruments have enabled certain violists, such as Don Ehrlich of the San Francisco Symphony, to play without misery. Before he made the switch, Ehrlich says, he was in severe pain from tendinitis at two places in his left elbow and feared "being badly injured."

SOME RAYS OF HOPE, PATHS TO GLORY

There are a few precious moments in the orchestral repertoire where the viola is the star, when the violin is absent and a violist is concertmaster. They include the sixth of Bach's *Brandenburg Concertos* and Brahms' Serenade No. 2 in A, Opus 16. And the solo viola repertoire is much slimmer than that for violin or cello. Mozart wrote two viola quintets and the *Sinfonia Concertante*, a concerto for violin and viola. William Walton wrote a viola concerto, as did Bela Bartok. Paul Hindemith, the German-born composer and violist who was on the faculty at Yale for many years, wrote perhaps the most for viola in the 20th century, including a concerto — so he could have pieces to perform.

In movies and TV, by contrast, the viola is used frequently to underscore sad or poignant moments. It's been said that if a baby dies, that's a viola solo. Goldsmith recalls the violinless score for the 1981 Richard Dreyfuss film *Whose Life Is It Anyway?* — "about a guy who's paralyzed and dying. He wants to kill himself." On another score, she says, she "played a viola solo when the baby dinosaur died." She had a big solo for a love scene in 1979's *Old Boyfriends*, which prompted her to thank composer David Shire "for thinking of the viola in this way, instead of in terms of death." But she was disheartened to learn: "Well, you see, when she's making love to this guy, she's really thinking about his dead brother, the one she really loved."

As for role models, Neufeld speaks for many violists when he lauds the late William Primrose, a Scot who was on the faculty at USC during the '60s and had a trio there with violinist Jascha Heifetz and cellist Gregor Piatigorsky. "When William Primrose came to the forefront," he says, "we had as our hero one of the world's outstanding instrumentalists." Dembow adds: "Primrose was in some ways even greater than Heifetz, because he sounded the way he did on the viola, which is much more difficult to do."

Pitelka agrees with a close violist friend whose goal was to have her instrument sound like Nat King Cole. "That has really stuck with me."

Meanwhile ...

What's the difference between a violist and Bin Laden hiding in an Afghan cave?

Everyone's looking for Bin Laden.

There doesn't seem to be any justice: Viola jokes just keep coming, even managing to stay au courant. But dedicated violists count on their devotion to their craft to protect them. Says Kato: "Playing well is the best revenge."

THINK SAX AND YOU PROBABLY WON'T THINK SYMPHONY

But it's just not 'Bolero' without one
March 13, 2005

MANY of today's symphony orchestra instruments have been around for centuries. The violin, for instance, dates to the 1500s and as a result has an enormous repertoire spanning 450 years. The saxophone, by contrast, wasn't invented until the mid-19th century, so it missed the Baroque and Classical periods entirely and, because it was known at first only in France, much of the Romantic era as well.

The saxophone is emphatically an orchestral instrument. Ravel's insinuating, repetitive *Bolero* is unthinkable without it. So is the achingly expressive portrayal of young love in Prokofiev's ballet *Romeo and Juliet*. Puccini, who used two saxophones in the orchestrations of his last opera, *Turandot*, is said to have considered the sound of the saxophone the closest of any instrument's to the human voice. Others hear in it the same soulfulness conveyed by the cello.

But then there was W.C. Fields, who supposedly observed that "the definition of a gentleman is a man who can play the saxophone but doesn't."

That crack points to classical saxophonists' plight: Most people probably think of the instrument in terms not of classical music but of jazz. The saxophone, after all, was the domain of such revered 20th century innovators as Charlie Parker — "Bird" — and John Coltrane.

Even Douglas Masek, one of the most in-demand classical players in Los Angeles, says that after he took up the sax as a 10-year-old, he was "listening to big band music and thought that was the way the instrument was supposed to sound. Then I heard a recording of the German saxophone virtuoso Sigurd Rascher. 'This is unbelievable,' I thought. 'Nobody plays saxophone like this.'"

Jim Rotter, another distinguished local player, tells a similar story: "I had been interested in jazz growing up because that's what I first heard — big band, then bebop, players like Bird and Coltrane. Classical music really fascinated me, but I didn't know the saxophone could do that.

"Then my high school band teacher gave me recordings of Sigurd Rascher and the Frenchman Marcel Mule, who was a concertizing saxophonist and Herbert von Karajan's saxophonist with the Berlin Philharmonic when a saxophonist was needed. I heard that instrument sing — just like an opera singer," he says.

The saxophone is a woodwind instrument made of brass. It was invented in the 1840s by the Belgian Adolphe Sax for military bands and orchestral use.

"Adolphe," as Masek calls him, "was going for a new instrument that would bridge the gap between the brass and woodwind sections. He came up with this instrument made of brass and thought he would try to put a mouthpiece on it, with a reed. He actually envisioned a saxophone section in the orchestra." In fact, there are six members of the saxophone family, though orchestral music is written primarily for soprano, alto and tenor.

Sax was an ambitious, brilliant man who had a knack for making friends and enemies alike. He improved a number of instruments, in particular the clarinet, and made the formerly unreliable bass clarinet into a standard component of the orchestra's woodwind section.

He obtained 35 patents, including one for a weapon intended to level cities — he called it the Saxocannon — and another for a fumigation box that interested Louis Pasteur. He was also a fine musician and the first saxophone instructor at the Paris Conservatory.

Somehow, though, the saxophone failed to cause the stir he had anticipated. Composer Hector Berlioz was a friend of Sax and a powerful proponent of the new instrument, but even he hardly wrote for it. Gary Foster, a veteran Los Angeles player who glides effortlessly between orchestral jobs and jazz gigs, speculates that the composers of Sax's day and later may have had an "aversion" to the saxophone.

"Why else would so many composers famous for broadening the orchestra, like Stravinsky, not include it?" Foster asks. "Why didn't Stravinsky include the saxophone in the "Ragtime" section of his *L'Histoire du Soldat*?" Stravinsky's alleged response when fellow composer Ingolf Dahl told him in 1949 that he was writing a saxophone concerto seems to bear this out: "Oh, that's nice. But the saxophone has always reminded me of a slimy, pink worm."

Some composers may have been ambivalent. Rotter recalls play-ing Lukas Foss' *Baroque Variations* a few years ago with the Los

Angeles Philharmonic, with Foss conducting. "We were rehearsing and we came to the big solo, and I played it and everybody shuffled their feet" — the musicians' sign of appreciation for a fellow player — "and Lukas stops, peers over the orchestra and says, 'What instrument is that?' I held it up and said, 'It's a soprano saxophone, maestro.' 'No, it's not. It's not crass and ugly enough.' So the next time 'round I just crassed and uglied the best I was capable of — and he got this big smile on his face."

Masek, who campaigns to get first-rate new music commissioned for his instrument, thinks certain composers may have ignored the saxophone simply because of "the lack of first-rate players." After Sax died in 1894, it wasn't until Rascher and Mule came on the scene in the 1930s that composers began writing for the saxophone in earnest.

In a bibliography of the instrument compiled by a student of Mule's, French saxophonist Jean-Marie Londeix, 14,000 works are listed, more than for any other woodwind instrument. But Londeix acknowledged to Rotter: "Maybe 1% or 2% are worth playing. And how many of those are masterpieces? Oh ... I don't want to even guess."

FILLING IN THE PERFORMANCE GAPS

According to Masek, "there is no orchestra in the world that employs a full-time saxophonist." So how do these rare beasts, classical saxophonists, stay alive? Between them, Masek and Rotter play for virtually every resident and visiting orchestra in the Southland.

Masek has also released several solo albums and recently signed with Centaur Records to record a three-CD set of music written for classical saxophone by Los Angeles-based composers. Additionally, he has a career as a soloist and this spring will play saxophone concertos in France, Switzerland and South Africa. And he's on the faculty at UCLA.

Rotter teaches at USC in addition to maintaining a full schedule as a contract player, but he is blunt with his students. "I tell them, 'You will not make your living as an orchestral saxophonist. Saxophonists today have to be able to cross over and do a bit of both'"— orchestral music and jazz.

The internationally renowned Gary Foster is the model of the saxophonist who straddles those worlds. Foster, who considers himself "primarily a woodwind doubler," majored in clarinet in college, although he says he "didn't particularly like it." But "there were no saxophone studios in American universities. You couldn't go to school to study classical saxophone. Today you can get a doctorate in saxophone performance."

In the '50s, Foster says, he came to L.A. just "to be a player." He has since accompanied Sinatra, Streisand, Rosemary Clooney, Johnny Mathis and Quincy Jones, to name a few, on a variety of instruments.

Last summer, when Los Angeles Opera offered Stephen Sondheim's *A Little Night Music*, he occupied the flute-clarinet chair. But when the company did the Weill opera *The Rise and Fall of the City of Mahagonny*, he held the saxophone chair, and he has played saxophone for John Adams when Adams conducted the Los Angeles Chamber Orchestra. Indeed, he has a particular appreciation for Adams, who "openly says, 'I love the saxophone.' "For L.A. Opera's production of Adams' *Nixon in China*, he was one of four saxophones, including a baritone. "That was a huge part. It had to have been an inch-and-a-half thick!"

Foster also fondly remembers working with the late film composer and arranger Peter Matz. "Peter would write above the saxophone part, 'More like the Mule [Marcel Mule] than the Bird [Charlie Parker] — more toward the classical. Or rather than 'This is a little jazzier,' he would write, 'More like the Bird than the Mule.'"

WHERE THE SAX SHINES

Composed in 1928, *Bolero* remains the work featuring saxophone that classical audiences probably know best. Nicknamed the "Bolero Boys," Masek and Rotter have sat patiently together through the first seven solos in the piece for more than 200 performances, keeping their reeds wet, their instruments' brass warm (so they won't be flat when they come in), counting 113 measures, or approximately 4 minutes, 45 seconds, before the tenor saxophone makes its entrance and an additional 31 measures, to approximately 5 1/2 minutes, before the soprano saxophone follows.

Apart from *Bolero*, the bread and butter of the classical saxophone remain Bizet's two *L'Arlesienne* suites, the first written in 1872, three years before his opera *Carmen*; Ravel's orchestration of Mussorgsky's *Pictures at an Exhibition* from 1922; Gershwin's 1924 *Rhapsody in Blue*; Kodaly's 1927 *Hary Janos* suite; Prokofiev's 1934 suite from *Lieutenant Kije*; and Rachmaninoff's 1941 *Symphonic Dances*.

These pieces may be few and far between, but they can't just be phoned in. Masek describes the situation: "Everything is solo. We have to sit and wait, sit and wait — sometimes for whole movements — before we play. Then we have to come in cold as a soloist. We play 16, maybe 24 bars, and then we're done. And there's no going back, trying to make up for something in another solo. 'Well, I didn't make a very good impression on that one. Maybe the next solo is going to be better.' We can't redeem ourselves by any means."

Foster sounds justifiably miffed: "There are many saxophone virtuosi who could easily be a James Galway, Richard Stoltzman or Yo-Yo Ma, performing saxophone repertoire with major orchestras, but that just doesn't happen. Works by Ibert, Glazunov, Milhaud and others would have excellent audience appeal.

"The Ibert Concertino, which was written for Sigurd Rascher, is a landmark piece. It was written in 1913, the same year as Stravinsky's *Rite of Spring*. It's been recorded, but I've never heard it with the Los Angeles Philharmonic. Unless you found a record store that had a buyer who liked classical saxophone, you wouldn't find a bin. Tower used to, but they don't have one anymore. I have lots of classical saxophone records, but in many cases the people self-produce and sell them themselves."

Meanwhile, the jazz saxophonist uses a different mouthpiece and is free to play out as a soloist, not needing to blend in with the rest of a woodwind section but soaring above everything else.

Still, if the saxophone was co-opted by jazz, Rotter is among the classical players who are gracious about the fact.

"It was also saved," he says. "I think if jazz hadn't come along, hadn't adopted the saxophone, it might have died out, like a lot of Sax's other inventions."

W.C. Fields obviously didn't know any concert saxophone players.

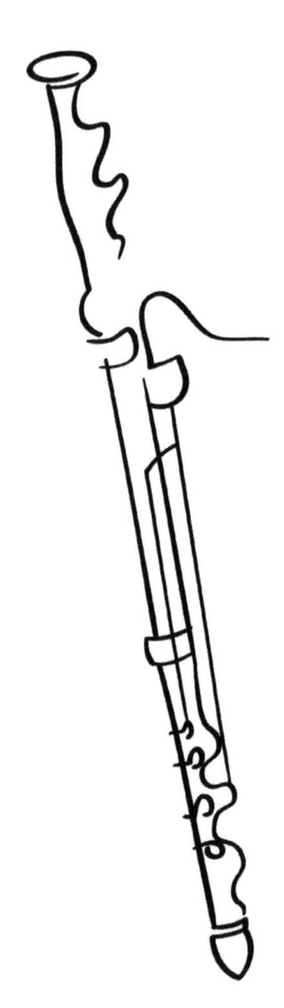

BASSOON: SYMPHONIC SPINE

Elusive but essential, the instrument gives its fellow woodwinds a bracing backbone
June 5, 2005

FRANK ZAPPA once wrote, "The bassoon is one of my favorite instruments. It has the medieval aroma — like the days when everything used to sound like that.... It's a great noise — nothing else makes that noise."

Nothing else resembles the bassoon either. It's the ungainly woodwind whose top you can glimpse sticking above the heads of most musicians in the orchestra (which typically has four bassoons) and is rimmed in metal or white. It's a double-reed, like the oboe and the English horn, but its reed is attached to a long, curved stem, which is attached in turn to an 8-foot-or-so tube folded back on itself. When taken apart, the whole thing has five sections.

John Steinmetz, a founding member of the local chamber group Xtet and principal bassoonist with Los Angeles Opera, explains: "Sometime in prehistory, human beings figured out that if you drilled holes along a tube and then covered up all those holes with your fingers, you could get the sound of the complete tube." Conversely, the fewer holes that were covered, the higher-pitched the result.

When it came to the bassoon, though, "because the tube is so long, the holes would be farther apart than the fingers can reach, so instrument makers drilled the holes at an angle. They come to the outside where your fingers can reach, and they go to the inside at the place that makes the correct note. Eventually, metal keys were added, so your finger can cover up a hole that is very far away."

Says Rose Corrigan, principal bassoonist with the Pacific Symphony and the Hollywood Bowl Orchestra: "Your left thumb alone has nine different functions."

OFF THE RADAR

Bassoons weigh about 7 1/2 pounds. Ken Munday, principal bassoonist with the Los Angeles Chamber Orchestra, balances his on one thigh using a Dutch-made device, while most of his compatriots, he says, "sit on a strap that is like a belt with a hook on the bottom, to hold it up." But apart from their instrument's physical challenges, bassoonists face what you might almost call an emotional hurdle: contending with obscurity.

As Munday puts it: "Being a bassoon player and the subject of investigation is like being one of those bottom feeders in a Jacques Cousteau special. You're going about your life scraping around in the dark and then bam! The lights come on, and you're blinded by unaccustomed curiosity that is usually reserved for finer fish."

Others echo that. Judith Farmer, principal bassoonist with the Santa Barbara Chamber Orchestra, recalls hearing her doctor order a prescription for her for physical therapy and telling an assistant to write "that she plays the cello, because nobody will know what a bassoon is." David Breidenthal, principal bassoonist with the Los Angeles Philharmonic, often tells strangers that he plays the clarinet — it seems easier than explaining what a bassoon is. Corrigan says: "I try to leave it at 'I'm a musician.' But sometimes the conversation gets to 'Oh, what instrument do you play?' When I say the bassoon, I can't tell you how many times people ask: 'Is it that oboe-like thing?'"

Yet Breidenthal, who has been with the Philharmonic for 40-plus years and became principal bassoonist in 1968, also displays the pride of an underdog. "The bassoon doesn't play as many solos as, say, the flute or clarinet," he says, "but the bassoon is the glue." Without the bassoon, the heart of the orchestra "would be just a mishmash between treble-clef instruments and the woodwinds."

"We hold the whole thing together. Aside from holding up the bottom of the four main woodwind instruments, we modify our colors, and in the process, suddenly it's not a flute and a bassoon, it's a 'flassoon.' And the combination of clarinet and bassoon is a 'bassinet.' The same thing with the oboe. It's our job to make these instruments into something altogether different. A good bassoon player has to have an ear for color and has to be a good ensemble player."

Says Munday: "You can create magic if you know what you're doing. Bassoon players are very intense about having good technique, playing solos and practicing things over and over, because it's difficult technically. But most of the time, it doesn't make a difference. It's a bit upsetting. You don't get many strokes for being a bassoon player. It's an instrument that is usually too soft except when it's too loud. The dynamic range is very narrow."

Asked about the price of a bassoon, Farmer laughs. "A high-end bassoon can cost as much as $35,000. I know for a string player that's not expensive, but for a wind instrument, it is — especially when you consider that we spend all this money to play an instrument nobody can hear!"

AN EXCLUSIVE CLUB

If there is a Sisyphean aspect to playing the bassoon, there is also an inherent perk. Right off the bat, Steinmetz says, he always got to play: "I didn't have to go into a room full of 50 flute players and be one of the three to be chosen. I was one of the two bassoon players when they needed four." In Steinmetz's case, his high school bassoon teacher also "encouraged me to compose, because the bassoon doesn't have a huge repertoire of solos or chamber music, and we don't often get the tune. So the need to create things became part of it for me." Among his works is a concerto for bassoon and orchestra, which premiered in 2003.

Still, Breidenthal — whose 2002 CD, *Bassoon Power*, includes several pieces he commissioned — says "today's symphony orchestras require almost limitless technical ability of the musicians," and bassoonists are no exception. Farmer, like Corrigan a USC faculty member who routinely prepares students to go out and audition for jobs, points out that not only is the bar constantly rising but, as more and more orchestras go under, more and more people are becoming musicians and vying for fewer and fewer positions.

She says Stravinsky's *Rite of Spring* is one of the essential pieces bassoon students must master, along with the overture to Mozart's *Marriage of Figaro*, which can feel like playing a bassoon concerto; Beethoven's Fourth Symphony; Tchaikovsky's Fourth, Fifth and Sixth symphonies; Ravel's *Bolero*; and Rimsky-Korsakov's *Scheherazade*.

The Rite of Spring, which begins with the high voice of a lone bassoon, premiered in 1913, so one might think that how to play that opening solo would be an open-and-shut case. Instead, the question continues to be debated. Says Steinmetz: "Stravinsky supposedly complained later in life that he should have written it even higher, because bassoon players were getting too good at it and the feeling he wanted was of a landscape bound by ice, where spring was struggling to break through. Sometimes, what the composer wants is for something to sound raw, uncivilized and difficult. But as a professional musician, you want to always seem civilized and accomplished."

Farmer recalls one conductor who complained, "It used to sound like a struggle. Now everybody plays it as if it's easy."

In general, Corrigan feels, the bassoon "has two very distinct characters: It can sound hollow in a haunting, almost eerie, melancholic way, and it can also sound animated, even silly." She thinks that if people recognize the sound at all, that's most likely thanks to the character of the Grandfather in Prokofiev's *Peter and the Wolf.*

When the Cleveland Orchestra appears in Orange County on Wednesday, concertgoers will hear another signature piece, Bartok's *Concerto for Orchestra,* whose second movement begins with a bassoon duet. (The Clevelanders will play *Bolero* the next night at Disney Hall.)

Steinmetz speaks fondly of Bach's bassoon parts "in many of his cantatas, his *St. Matthew Passion* and the B minor Mass." He also mentions Vivaldi, "who taught at an all-girls school in Venice and wrote at least 38 bassoon concertos. And they're hard music." The players, he says, "must've been really good." Farmer, for her part, articulates every bassoonist's sentiment: "Probably our most beautiful work is the Mozart Bassoon Concerto. And we're so grateful to have it."

Steinmetz adds that the bassoon "is used very effectively in opera, not just in *The Marriage of Figaro*, and for different effects. For instance, in Donizetti's screwball comedy *The Elixir of Love*, the tenor love aria is introduced by the harp and bassoon. In Richard Strauss' opera *Die Frau Ohne Schatten*, the bassoon plays a very low, mysterious and gloomy solo when two important characters are locked in a dungeon."

In his sunny music room in La Crescenta, Munday lovingly surveys what he calls his "gaggle" of bassoons — among them a contrabassoon, or double bassoon, whose case resembles a casket more than an instrument container. He sifts through numerous reeds, separating them according to the Baroque, Classical and modern periods. "It's a really dorky instrument," he observes. "When you first look at it, if you have a chance to play the guitar, a chance to play other stuff, why the bassoon? Well, if you seek a certain frequency, it provides that."

Zappa agreed: "Some people crave baseball — I find this unfathomable — but I can easily understand why a person could get excited about playing a bassoon."

DOUBLE BASS: ALWAYS THE HEAVY

Whether its tones are signaling dread or enforcing the ensemble's pitch, it makes an unmistakable mark. Just don't try to fly with one
March 5, 2006

HEARD the one about the double bass player from the Metropolitan Opera who takes a night off to attend a performance of *Carmen*? Afterward, he rushes backstage to see his colleagues from the bass section. "You know where we have those long plonk, plonk, plonk, plonks?" he exclaims. "You wouldn't believe what the violins are doing!" And he starts humming the Toreador Song.

Yes, violists may be the orchestra musicians who are traditionally the butt of jokes, but Los Angeles Philharmonic principal bassist Dennis Trembly is "surprised that viola jokes didn't land on bass players." That brand of humor, he believes, originates with players of "smaller instruments with more virtuosic possibilities. You can play more notes per second on a smaller instrument. We play fewer notes, so they may feel we're not working as hard."

Trembly's fellow Philharmonic bass player David Moore

observes: "The sound of one bass or even a bass section is probably the most obscure instrumental sound in the entire orchestra. There are very few instances that you can even point to in the repertoire. It's a challenge to prepare students for auditions because it's not like saying to a violinist working on the Brahms concerto, 'Pick up a dozen recordings. Go to iTunes so you can hear some examples of great solo violin playing.'"

Yet whether it's referred to as a double bass, a contrabass, a string bass, an upright bass, an acoustic bass, a bass viol, a bass fiddle or even a bass violin, this mighty stringed instrument is indispensable to a full orchestra, which typically has a minimum of eight. The way Sue Ranney, principal bassist of the Los Angeles Chamber Orchestra, sees it, the bass is "the foundation of the orchestra. Pitch really starts from the bottom up. It's a problem when everybody just plays his or her own pitch — you need to fall down to that bottom. We're the basis of the pitch, we're the basis of the rhythm. Bach continuo parts are the heart and soul of moving music forward. To me, Bach is what the bass is all about."

To many other people, the bass is the lowest-toned instrument in the violin family. Technically, though, it's an offspring of not only the violin but the viola da gamba, an early stringed instrument held between the knees and comparable in range to the cello. Four hundred years after being perfected, the violin retains the same shape, it still has four strings, and it's still tuned in the musical intervals known as fifths. The basses in use today, though, reflect two traditions: the flat-backed, rounded-body shape of the viola da gamba family and the curve-backed, more-pointed-corners shape of the violin. And to make matters even more confusing, basses with elements from each tradition abound.

Moreover, the instrument's various incarnations have had three, four and five strings. Los Angeles Opera principal bassist David

Young explains: "Throughout the 19th century, there were many tunings and they were regional, so you play music and you try to interpolate what the composer really wanted."

An average bass stands from 6 to 6 1/2 feet tall, is 26 inches across at its widest part and is 8 inches deep. It can easily weigh 25 to 35 pounds. And because of its massiveness, people tend to think of it as "a man's instrument." Thirty years ago, Ranney remembers, a musicians' contractor explained to her why she couldn't possibly be a principal player: "Conductors want to see a strong guy back there." Says Moore: "I think the size of it gives people the mistaken impression that you have to be a brute to play it. But it's a misconception, especially these days, with the advancements of the technical abilities of players and a more thorough understanding of body usage."

Consider Lisa Gass, a rail-thin freelance bassist and member of the Pasadena Symphony who studied instrument making at the Violin Making School of America in Salt Lake City. Gass knows the bass inside out. She worked as the bass repair person in a violin shop in Los Angeles for 13 years and in 1997 opened her own business, LA Bassworks. The second floor has one room devoted to "all the really broken ones."

"In the past," says Gass, "the sheer size of the bass dictated that students had to begin when they were older and bigger. Young children were channeled into violin because there were small instruments." However, because the Suzuki method of teaching youngsters to play musical instruments now includes the bass, "small basses are more available and desirable, even for little girls. Basses go all the way down to one-tenth size." All the same, Moore points out, "there are still more men than women in many bass sections, unlike the other strings, which are 50-50 or maybe even more than 50%. It may very well be the last bastion of male dominance in the strings in the orchestra."

Ironically, it was a female bass player, Orin O'Brien, who in 1966 became the first woman admitted into the men-only club a.k.a. the New York Philharmonic. According to Trembly, O'Brien's method of getting around Manhattan was well known: "She'd put the bass behind a streetlight or lamppost, out of sight, stand at the curb, get a cab, open both doors and run and get her bass before the cab driver had a chance to drive away."

A SKILL WITH SOME BAGGAGE

Transportation is a big deal to bass players. And the problems begin from the get-go, when as Ranney puts it, "the carpool mom doesn't want to take you because the bass might hurt the car uphol-stery." In fact, to get a bass from anyplace to anyplace else, a player has to wrestle with the sheer clumsiness of the instrument. Ranney continues: "They're not ridiculously heavy, but they're awkward because the weight is out front. You have to lift it to put it into the car, muscle it around, lift it to take it out." She remembers a day early in her career when "I was walking to the Libbey Bowl at Ojai, carrying my bass, a stool, a music stand and my clothes. A guy walking toward me asked: 'Got a match?'" Life improved enormously, about 10 or 15 years ago, she says, when a wheel was invented that enables players to roll their instruments rather than carry them.

When traveling, Trembly prefers flying with the Philharmonic to flying solo: "They palletize the instruments, putting the basic trunks in a larger container that can be lifted with a forklift onto the airplane." He also looks back fondly to the '60s, "when you could pay half fare for a domestic flight, put the bass in the bulk-head seat next to the window and sit next to the bass." On one such trip, Moore remembers "being served two meals because my bass was entitled to a breakfast sandwich."

But if flying has changed for everyone since 2001, it's become next to impossible for bass players. Trembly laments: "When you want to ship an instrument to be repaired in another state or to import one to try out to consider buying it, you have to deal with Homeland Security to let you ship it without you being on the plane with it. I once lent one of my basses to a Canadian group playing at LACMA because the U.S. wouldn't let them fly the bass in. The airlines can be very arbitrary. Some airlines won't accept them as extra baggage at all."

Moore is specific about what's at stake. "Most of the safety of the instrument is in the quality of the case and knowing how to pack it properly," he says. "But you'll get to the airport and the security people will want to open, unpack and repack the case, and you, the bass player, are not supposed to touch it." He says that more than once, he's felt like telling transportation security employees, "Let's go into another room. I'm happy to strip naked and do this for you, but if it doesn't get put in right, I could get there and the thing could be irreparably damaged."

He shakes his head in bafflement: "If you were to take any person off the street and say, 'I have a case that has a wide end and a narrow end and a flat side and an angled side. You're going to send it down a ramp — how do you put it on?,' everyone would say, 'Flat side down, big side first.' " But despite his drawing "arrows and signs indicating which side is up and writing 'Fragile' all over, I can't tell you how many times you see it coming down neck first, lying on the bridge."

Another problem for bass players is that buying a string instrument and bow is not like buying a pair of shoes. They don't come in matching sets, and finding the right bow can often be the more difficult task. Plus, choosing a bass bow has an extra twist. There are two types, French and German, and they require two distinctly different bow holds. Gripping a French bow is similar to holding a cello bow. The thumb is underneath the bow stick, the fingers lean over from above. But the German bow, descended from the Baroque bow, is held with the palm facing the ceiling — in other words, underhanded.

Gass remarks that sometimes "people with hand problems who play French come in to get a German bow, or vice versa. You can't just switch — you have to work at it. Personally, I can't keep a German bow on the strings." Conversely, Trembly confesses that when he briefly tried a French bow, "I had grooves in my thumb, was black and blue on the side of my index finger from pressing, pinching, bad friction, and had no power in my stroke. I even dropped the bow a couple of times." Is it possible to hear the difference? According to Trembly, "One has suspicions."

SHYING FROM THE SPOTLIGHT

As that joke about the bass player attending *Carmen* indicates, basses rarely get the melody. Or as Trembly puts it: "In the orchestra, you've got Britten's *Young Person's Guide*, Prokofiev's *Lieutenant Kije*, Stravinsky's *Pulcinella*, the Elephant in Saint-Saëns' *Carnival of the Animals* and various symphonic repertoire here and there. But for the most part, we don't play alone a lot, and when we suddenly do, it's kind of unnerving. It's an unaccustomed prominence which can make one insecure."

Ultimately, though, Trembly enjoys the spotlight. He is grateful to bass soloist Bertram Turetzky, "who recently retired from UCSD, for commissioning over 150 pieces for solo bass or chamber music with bass in it." Former Philharmonic composer in residence John

Harbison, Trembly adds, is writing a Concerto for Double Bass and Orchestra, "which will be performed by various orchestras. I am going to perform it with the Los Angeles Philharmonic the week of Thanksgiving."

Young of L.A. Opera, who is also on the faculty of the Colburn School of Performing Arts, has a special fondness for the bass parts in Verdi. "In Othello's entrance into Desdemona's bedchamber," he says, "the basses play this moaning 'thing,' which step by step builds up to his determination to kill her. In the very beginning of *Rigoletto*, there is dialogue going on above a melody played in octaves with one cello and one bass. With that extra deep darkness in it, there is the foreboding. You know that Rigoletto's daughter, whom he's protected from the Count, is going to get it, it's going to turn out the worst it could, and it does. That's the whole opera's tension. It's set up right there with the bass."

Moore, for his part, argues that many bass players "want to be part of a group, something larger than themselves. Few go into it because they want to be center stage." But there have been exceptions, and he notes that a number of them, responding to the dearth of bass music, have written music for themselves. Domenico Dragonetti, a virtuoso bass player whose career spanned the latter half of the 18th and the first half of the 19th centuries, apparently inspired Beethoven. Giovanni Bottesini was a hotshot in the 19th century who also composed pieces for himself.

In the 20th century, Serge Koussevitzky, originally a bass player but better known as conductor of the Boston Symphony, also wrote for the bass. In the 1960s, native Californian Gary Karr emerged as a superstar among bass players; Young goes so far as to say that Karr "should be considered the driving pioneering force who almost single-handedly elevated the bass to a solo instrument from a rare oddity." And today there's Edgar Meyer, composer and bass player, the Yo-Yo Ma of the bass. Ask any bassist and she or he will almost immediately run out of superlatives to characterize Meyer, who will premiere his Double Bass Concerto No. 2 with the Los Angeles Chamber Orchestra on April 8 and 9.

In the end, the bass remains a quirky, unstandardized instrument whose players must act unceasingly as its advocates. Ranney puts her bass "out there" in her trio, L'eau, with a bassoonist and a violist. They play transcriptions as well as music they've commissioned. Bass players have sometimes been characterized as party animals, which may be stretching things. But they certainly have a sense of humor, as the PR for L'eau makes clear. The group, it says, performs works from "the Dark Ages to the Current Recession."

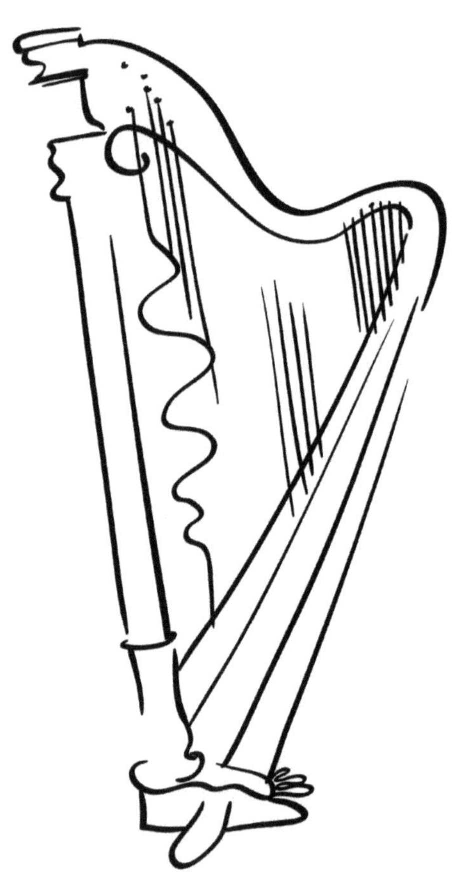

THE HARP: HEAVEN FOR A PLUCKY FEW

For players, the instruments set the gold standard with an ethereal "carpet of sound"
April 22, 2007

ANYONE attending a symphony concert can spot the gorgeous, gleaming harp, even from the last row of the last balcony. Children and adults alike gasp at the size of it, at its sparkling gold crown towering above the musicians. Lou Anne Neill, principal harpist of the Los Angeles Philharmonic for the last 24 years, remembers the first time she glimpsed a harp in the back of an orchestra. "I couldn't see the strings from where I was sitting," she says. "I just saw hands move through the air, and these beautiful sounds were coming out of the instrument."

Neill loves the harp's "plucked sound, which really does take you into a very beautiful world." Its players "sit behind the instrument getting it full-force on our shoulder." Marcia Dickstein, a busy L.A. freelance harpist, also relishes "the physical sensation as the vibration goes through your body, since you wrap yourself in sound."

"Being in the middle of the orchestra is the best seat in the house," Dickstein says. "People should pay to be where I am."

The fact is, however, that though the harp has existed all over the globe as a solo instrument, in one form or another, since ancient times, it wasn't until 1810 that a Frenchman, piano maker Sebastien Erard, invented the double-action pedal harp — the standard 80-pound, 46- or 47-string orchestral instrument we know today. It has seven pedals, one for each note in the conventional Western scale, that tighten the strings so their pitch is sharp, flat or natural. As Neill puts it: "The left hand is bass, the right hand treble. All the chromatic capabilities are in your feet."

Before Erard's invention, harps simply weren't used in orchestral writing. "Women played them in salons," says Dickstein.

Even now, notes Rachel Van Voorhees, on sabbatical from her position as principal harpist with the Louisiana Philharmonic, "I can go through a whole season where I play every single concert, and then I might go through a season where they play a Mozart or Beethoven cycle and I don't play at all, because those particular composers didn't write orchestral parts for the harp. Most of the music that involves orchestral harp was written after 1850. For most people, it's easiest to envision that the music of Debussy, Faure and the Impressionistic composers forward is where you'll find the wonderful harp parts."

As Neill sees it, "the 20th century has been our time. Stravinsky wrote a lot of very important harp parts. He didn't necessarily write well for the instrument, but they're brilliant, so all harpists try to play them the way he wanted."

Moreover, according to Metropolitan Opera principal harpist Deborah Hoffman, "Now that the harp is so developed and there are no limitations to chromatic possibilities, composers such as Elliott Carter, John Adams, John Harbison, Philip Glass and numerous others write pieces, often very difficult, where the harp is used prominently." Hoffman recently played in the Met's premiere of Tan Dun's *The First Emperor*, which, she says, "in contrast to the typical lush, rich and warm glissandi, used the instrument in a more percussive manner, creating a more aggressive, harsher, even brutal tone."

STRENGTH COMES INTO PLAY

Despite the harp's size and heft, Dickstein reports that "you go to a harp convention, it's 90% women." Says Van Voorhees: "We all have this image of a dainty female playing the harp, but quite honestly, it takes a tremendous amount of upper-body strength, physical coordination and stamina, and men would have a natural advantage." In fact, it was a man, Harpo Marx of the Marx Brothers, who was probably responsible for introducing more people to the harp than anyone else. "When you see him play," says Hoffman, "it's absolutely magical. He goes into this world. He's not funny anymore."

Whether male or female, harpists seem to agree that strumming the instrument is the least of their worries. Pushing the right pedal at the right time is far more complex, a bit like driving with a stick shift. Says Van Voorhees: "If I'm in the key of C and the pedals are all in one spot and it modulates to the key of G, then while I'm playing I'm moving the F pedal to F sharp. That affects all the Fs on the harp. On the organ, when you move a pedal it's just for that single note." To ease the burden, Neill explains, "the strings are color-coded, because they feel the same. Cs are red, Fs black and everything in between is beige. We're looking at the harp, at the colors, at the music, at the conductor."

In the U.S., there are two primary schools of harp playing. One, codified by the French harpist and composer Henriette Renie (1875-1956), is known as the French method. It was popularized in the U.S. by a student of Renie's, Marcel Grandjany. The other system is named after its chief exponent, another French harpist and composer, Carlos Salzedo (1885-1961).

"Everything about them is different," says Dickstein, "even the way you read and mark music. For instance, you can mark pedalings within, below or above the staff — in French, English or pedal diagrams. There's no right way. Salzedo created a whole system of notation that is not something you would see in general notation. It's very specific to his writing."

As a child, Hoffman studied with a Salzedo teacher in the winter and a Grandjany teacher in the summer. "My elbows would be up during the winter, down during the summer," she recalls. "Salzedo players keep their elbows up in the air to make these big gesticulations, which they think helps to bring out the sound. It was very awkward for me and didn't feel good. I developed tendinitis from the tension of switching. When I was growing up, though, it seemed that Salzedo people occupied the big jobs. They were really strong players who seemed to have these gigantic sounds." Still, Hoffman wound up attending the Juilliard School, where she studied the French method with the renowned Susann McDonald, a student of Renie.

Such distinctions seem to be waning. Barbara Allen, a harpist with the orchestra of American Ballet Theatre, thinks so. Her most important teacher, a Salzedo student, "felt you can't say somebody has to have their wrist at this angle or their elbow at this angle, because everyone's different. She was very concerned about people developing their own style. I think that's happening more and more."

Hoffman sees the harp in any symphony setting as "adding a

certain color, a carpet of sound." In opera, she says, it's "accompaniment for the voice. Sometimes you may not know that the harp is playing, but you would certainly know it's not there if you didn't hear it."

IN BALLET'S SPOTLIGHT

But, as Allen can attest, the harp's greatest prominence is in 19th century ballet scores. One of three sisters who are accomplished harpists, Allen had just finished a stint with the San Francisco Symphony when she was approached 17 years ago about auditioning for the harp spot with ABT.

She took the audition, she says, despite having had her first child just days before, "really just to get back into shape. I had two weeks to learn the repertoire," her stiffest competition turned out to be a jackhammer on the floor above "and I broke a string." Nevertheless, she got the gig — without having a clue about the harp's workload in ballet.

"Next to the solo violin, it's the most featured instrument," she says. "On average, there are 45 solos per season, within two months. While any major orchestra with a harp audition is going to have *Nutcracker* on the list, that's about it. Unless you're in a company, you're not going to be doing the standards: *Corsaire, Bayadere, Don Q, Raymonda, Sleeping Beauty, Swan Lake.* It's pretty stressful."

Allen remembers breaking into a sweat some years ago as she worked to replace a broken string within a nine-minute tacet, or period of silence, she had during "Swan Lake." The string needed to be stretched as much as possible so it would be in tune for her cadenza — what Neill refers to as "the mother of all cadenzas," which leads into the Prince's first pas de deux with the Swan Queen. Consequently, Allen was flabbergasted at intermission when the conductor's wife said, "Barbara, I never knew how interesting it was to watch you change a string!" Apparently "everyone in that first and second tier could see me."

For the moment, Van Voorhees has settled in L.A. to work with Neill, in association with the Young Musicians Foundation, running their brainchild, the Harp in Our Public Schools Project. They have 38 third- and fourth-graders at Moffett Elementary School in Lennox. Some of the kids played at a Target during the holidays to thank the retailer for donating money to the school. In February, they performed for Dana Gioia, chairman of the National Endowment for the Arts, and Rep. Jane Harman (D-Venice).

The students in Lennox are learning on Dusty Strings' Ravenna folk harps, which have 26 strings, not 40-odd, and cost $745 as opposed to the $50,000 that the harps audiences see on the concert stage and in orchestra pits frequently command. But Neill, who has taught at Moffett for several years, says the lustrous vision of a full-size harp remains the gold standard for her students.

At the beginning of each group's first class, she tells her pupils that "they're going to get to play the gold harp at the end of the lesson. I save about 15 minutes and, with the help of the teacher, we line them up and they sit down and I show them how to play glissando. The look on their faces is priceless."

ACCORDION: HOLDS A LOFTY PLACE

Ranked just above the kazoo in some musical circles, the accordion has had a long-standing and illustrious past outside the U.S. Maybe someday it'll get a little respect
April 20, 2008

MOST people think of the accordion, if they think of it at all, as a social instrument, wheezing out polkas and folk tunes. The sound of it brings to mind French cafes, Mexican plazas, German beer gardens, Argentine nightclubs. Nick Ariondo, perhaps the premier accordionist in Los Angeles, notes that the instrument's portability and its ability to play "everything: melody, chords and accompaniment" have made it popular all over the world.

But the accordion is not just an instrument of the people. As Samuel Zyman, a New York composer and a faculty member at the Juilliard School, puts it: "There is a significant serious classical repertoire written for accordion, plus an extensive catalog of transcriptions of piano, organ and orchestral works."

Even Tchaikovsky used the concertina, a sort of hexagonal

accordion, in one of his orchestral suites. Prokofiev included the accordion in his *Cantata for the Anniversary of the October Revolution*. And a quick look at the list of the dozens of works commissioned by the other AAA — the American Accordionists' Assn. — reveals music by Henry Cowell, David Diamond, Lukas Foss, Virgil Thomson and Ernest Krenek.

Like hem lengths, though, the accordion has been subject to fashion. Because it was cheaper and easier to make room for than a piano, there was a period a few decades back when children all over the world, particularly little boys, played the accordion. They included Zyman, 51, who began music lessons in his native Mexico City studying the instrument.

"The accordion is an amazing instrument," says Ariondo, 58, who is also a composer and arranger. "It's powerful, but it's also delicate and sensitive. The public, when they really listen to it, are totally amazed. But let's face it, the serious-minded people are reluctant about it."

Indeed, nowadays the prevailing attitude may best be reflected by the popular bumper sticker "Use an accordion — go to jail."

However you view it, the accordion can seem like a contradiction in terms. Says Ariondo: "When you see the piano side of it, complete with white and black notes, you expect to see hammers, not valves. But this is a push-and-pull reed instrument. When you pull out on the accordion, you're sucking air into it. It sounds like a harmonica. The bellows is like the bow on the violin. It's very difficult to master."

The surface of most accordions looks like mother-of-pearl, but actually, Ariondo says, "it's celluloid, a very fine, high-profile plastic that's very flammable. This thing is around a fire, boom — it's going to go up. But underneath is all wood. On a standard professional accordion, there are 448 reeds made of Swedish steel. They are attached to wooden reed blocks on the inside of the accordion and covered by the bellows. Tuning an accordion is a veteran's job: Waxed-in reed plates are removed, cleaned and rewaxed; reed tongues must be filed to sharpen or flatten the pitch; and valve leathers need replacing. There are thousands of parts to this instrument. When I do the L.A. Opera or a concert, I have an extra one on the side, just in case something weird happens."

Explaining why the accordion has made it into the classical world, Zyman notes that "like the organ, the accordion has different registrations that can make it sound like many different instruments, such as the flute, clarinet and bassoon, or even like an orchestral tutti. Moreover, the accordion has the ability to sustain the sound, to produce highly effective crescendos and to create a very expressive vibrato. None of this is possible on the piano." Ariondo regards it as a "mini-orchestra." All of which may make the accordion sound similar to a synthesizer, a creation from the end of the 20th century. But the first instrument called the accordion was patented in Vienna in 1829.

Playing the accordion can even suggest some chore from the Industrial Revolution. "If you don't have the right training," Ariondo says, "and you start pulling the bellows the wrong way, you can mess up the tendons in your arm. It's very strenuous on your whole system. Everybody has to find ways to keep themselves from wearing out, a different angle."

There are also, he points out, numerous varieties of accordion: "piano-accordions, concertina, the bandoneon" — made famous by composer-bandoneonist Astor Piazolla, who took the Argentine tango to a new level — "and the bayan, from Russia." Zyman offers: "Perhaps the two most distinct kinds are one with a piano-like keyboard and another with buttons instead of keys for the right hand."

THE KEY IS VERSATILITY

The accordion is by no means universally ridiculed. Consider that, as played by Frank Marocco, it was the star of Michael Giacchino's score for last year's hit animated film *Ratatouille.*

Marocco, 77, is widely regarded as one of the great jazz accordionists and is the town's top accordionist on studio dates, which might require him on any given day to play jazz, folk, pop or classical. He started the accordion at age 7.

Like Zyman, who at age 14 won a national accordion competition in Mexico, Marocco eventually "won a big contest" and "started playing a few jobs around town, weddings and birthday parties. I went on the road with my trio," leaving his native Joliet, Ill., and wound up playing "the Vegas circuit — Las Vegas, Reno and Tahoe — where I learned to play almost every standard ever written: George Gershwin, Cole Porter, Jerome Kern, Duke Ellington."

In 1959, he landed in Los Angeles, where he decided he had to "settle down and figure out how to make a living."

"It was a very scary time," he says. "Here I was in this big city, and I didn't know anyone. The accordion was still popular. There were accordion studios around, so I took a job teaching. Los Angeles is a small town where musicians are concerned. They find out about each other. All of a sudden, someone said, 'There's a new accordion player in town, he's really good.' So I started getting a Saturday night job, a Sunday job, a Friday night. Pretty soon, I was working all the time, through word of mouth. I did a little bit of studio work during that time, but not a lot. There were guys ahead of me who were already established."

Still, in 1965 Marocco was one of two accordionists on Maurice Jarre's wildly popular orchestral score for the film *Doctor Zhivago.*

The other was veteran Carl Fortina, who was enjoying a successful career playing for various TV series, including *Gunsmoke* and *Bonanza*. Then, in the late '70s, when Fortina succeeded another accordionist, Dominic Frontiere, as music contractor at Paramount Studios, the door into television opened for Marocco.

One of his early experiences was doing *The Waltons*. Composer Alexander Courage "would write for a small woodwind section that would have the flute, oboe, clarinet, bassoon and accordion. And he would write me little clusters — two-, three-, four-note chords — to blend in with the other woodwinds, so he had a nice, full woodwind section."

Today, Marocco is busier than ever. In the three *Pirates of the Caribbean* films, "I played three different instruments — accordion, bass accordion and musette. Michael Giacchino likes the accordion, so he wrote a lot of stuff for me to play."

Yet Marocco observes that the accordion today is much more common in Europe than in the U.S. "In Germany alone, there are 3,000 accordion orchestras, with 30 or 40 players each. In America, we're lucky if we have 3,000 accordion players."

FALLING INTO THE WRONG HANDS

If a U.S. accordionist refers to his instrument as a "stomach Steinway," "organ grinder" or "squeezebox," it can be in a spirit of gentle self-deprecation. Often, however, "squeezebox" is not a compliment. And Marocco believes the reason is simple: "Most accordion players don't play it the way it should be played. For every good player, there are 100 poor ones." Part of the problem, Marocco acknowledges, is that "unlike the violin, with a few lessons you can immediately play a simple little song on the accordion. Unfortunately, most of the accordion players never took it much further. They learned to play a little polka, a little waltz, a march, and they're satisfied."

Among Los Angeles cognoscenti, by contrast, Marocco is considered a superb musician who just happens to play the accordion. In addition to his studio work, he plays in a group with L.A. Chamber Orchestra French hornist Richard Todd and with drummer Peter Erskine, bass player Michael Valerio and pianist Billy Childs. "I get a chance to have a lot of fun, besides making a living. Now it's no longer about the money."

Marocco enjoys the feeling of the instrument against him: "You're breathing when you use the bellows." He likens the player's control to that of a singer — which may help explain why the accordion has been used to provide accompaniment in a number of operas. With L.A. Opera, Ariondo has played for Kurt Weill's *The Threepenny Opera* and *Rise and Fall of the City of Mahagonny*. In the company's production of Samuel Barber's *Vanessa*, he was onstage with violinist Armen Anassian playing an atonal waltz.

Then there is British bad boy Thomas Ades' *Powder Her Face,*" which Ariondo characterizes as "quite risque. I did it at USC, with the Long Beach Opera, and again in San Francisco with Kent Nagano. It is written for a chamber ensemble of 17 instruments. Ades had me play with everybody in the chamber ensemble. He understands that when you combine accordion with other instruments, magic starts to happen. I had to practice that thing so much to make things work. There are difficult concertos, like the Paul Kreston one, but as far as chamber music is concerned, that one takes the cake."

Like Marocco, Ariondo plays in smaller ensembles as well. On May 22, he'll be part of a concert at the Goethe-Institut Los Angeles showcasing his arrangements for accordion, viola and soprano of music by Beethoven, Schubert, Mendelssohn and others.

Every accordionist is used to people bringing up Gary Larson's *The Far Side* cartoon of a newcomer to heaven receiving a harp while, down below, the devil forks over an accordion. But like a hem length on the way out, that point of view may once again be growing dated. Just Google "accordion." One of the more than 8 million results is the website www.AccordionHeaven.com.

SECOND VIOLINISTS: FIRST-CLASS MUSICIANS

Supporting the first violinist in an orchestra or a chamber group requires 'a different kind of virtuosity,' but no less proficiency
May 17, 2009

DAN Nobuhiko Smiley is principal second violinist for the San Francisco Symphony. He laughs at his title: "Sounds like an oxymoron. How can you be a principal and second at the same time?"

Not every concertgoer realizes that the sea of violins in a symphony orchestra consists of two distinct sections. Likewise, there are two violins in a string quartet. In both cases, the first violins generally "knock out the high melodies," as Smiley puts it, while the second violins handle the accompaniment.

Take Verdi's operas or Tchaikovsky's ballets. While the first violins play the themes that people go out of the theater humming, the second violins most often provide the oom-pah-pahs.

"Playing second fiddle" may connote being second best, but the preparation for playing first or second violin is exactly the same. "You learn concertos and the brilliant, virtuosic stuff," Smiley explains.

Glenn Dicterow is the concertmaster of the New York Philharmonic — the first violin of the first violin section. He cites his father as an illustration that second violin does not mean second rate. Harold Dicterow was a child prodigy who, according to his son, was hired by Pierre Monteux for the first violin section of the San Francisco Symphony when he was 17 — the youngest person ever hired in that orchestra. When he enlisted in the Army a couple of years later, he was promised his spot back after World War II ended. Instead, he joined the Los Angeles Philharmonic as principal second violinist. He stayed there for 52 years.

"There may be a second violin mentality," Dicterow says, "but I am not aware of it. My father would sometimes make jokes that they never go out of first position" — the fingering that beginning violinists start with — "but that is not true. Actually, most orchestral repertoire has extremely difficult second violin material. Zubin Mehta considered my father one of the truly great orchestral section leaders."

According to Margaret Batjer, concertmaster of the Los Angeles Chamber Orchestra, "often openings in orchestras dictate which section a person will audition for. It is often not 'their' choice but a matter of practicality."

On the other hand, Dicterow says that although all violinists auditioning for the New York Philharmonic prepare a first violin part, "violinists hired by major orchestras usually go directly into the second violin section. Our string sections have rotation, so all second violinists actually end up playing in the firsts at some point during every season — all except the frozen players, who sit on the first two stands of the seconds."

If there are vacancies in the first section in the N.Y. Philharmonic, there are always "in-house" auditions first. Only if no one from within the orchestra is chosen is a vacancy advertised and open to outsiders.

WHERE TO SIT?

In all symphony orchestras, the location of the first violin section is set in stone: It is always on the conductor's left. And the most common placement of the second violins fits with their "lesser-than" status: They're buried behind the first violins and the cello section is placed directly opposite the first violins. In this configuration, the second violins sit next to the violas — which, considering that these two sections constitute the "inner" voices, means that their being sandwiched between the treble and bass is helpful.

But that is not always the case. There are certain conductors who use the European set-up, placing the second violin section directly across from the first violins, with the cellos and violas between them. Los Angeles Opera music director James Conlon always uses this format; Esa-Pekka Salonen favored it during his last two seasons as music director of the Los Angeles Philharmonic. Dmitry Sitkovetsky, who is both a solo violinist and a conductor, believes "it's good to have the cellos on the inside because then they project."

Smiley notes that visually, "it's very impressive, having the violins flanking both sides of the stage. My section has mixed feelings about it. I kind of like it because it brings out a dynamic dualism between the violins and at the same time the equality between the first and seconds."

Although Sitkovetsky believes the latter setup works better with a chamber orchestra, he too feels there are definite benefits, particularly for the second violins: "Immediately it exposes them, makes them uncomfortable, because they are far from the firsts. But it energizes them, and they don't feel so invisible and unappreciated."

Smiley acknowledges that he can't help but "judge both conductors and composers on how they treat second violinists. There are wonderful composers who will give the second violinists really interesting parts — not perfunctory, but they will highlight and can be very subtle in the way that they accompany or imitate or embellish the line."

Sitkovetsky agrees. "Richard Strauss, in *Ein Heldenleben*, very rare in the repertoire, puts the seconds higher than the firsts and gives them the theme, which is unusual."

Smiley says that "some conductors are more aware than others of that. It's not uncommon when we're playing a melody with the first violins for a conductor to say, 'The first violins are naturally more brilliant here. Firsts play a little bit less, seconds a little bit more. I want to hear that lower octave.' And that's what gives it that depth, and the richness pops out."

QUARTET FUNCTION

In a string quartet, the second violinist's role is much the same as an orchestra second. Emerson String Quartet violinist Eugene Drucker explains that the second violinist has to lead or coordinate the lower three instruments — second violin, cello and viola in supporting the first violinist. "Sometimes, he or she has to provide a secure underpinning for the first violin in octave passages," Drucker said.

In the Emerson, Drucker and his fellow violinist, Philip Setzer, trade off the first and second parts. Says Drucker: "Twenty-plus years ago, when Phil Setzer and I formed a student quartet at the Juilliard School, it was fairly common practice for the violinists to switch. I didn't know of any professional groups that did it previously. We evolved quite gradually into a professional group, so there was never a point at which we said to each other, 'OK, now it's time to get serious and establish fixed positions.'"

Drucker notes that in quartet writing, the second violin part may not be necessarily easier but is "less exposed." Consequently there is less stress in the job, and "it can be very gratifying if it suits his/her temperament and if the entire group gets along well personally and musically."

Playing second violin in an orchestra is, for the most part, less demanding technically and requires less practice at home. Still, many violinists who play second violin in an orchestra, like Smiley, keep their chops up by playing first violin in chamber ensembles or when doing studio work. So all that time and energy spent acquiring first-rate technique is definitely utilized.

Occasionally, says Sitkovetsky, "you get a star second violinist." Such was the case with the Budapest Quartet's Alexander "Sasha" Schneider. Yet his fame did not come simply from his being a very dynamic presence in the ensemble, but because he did an enormous amount to promote music and help students. Says Sitkovetsky: "He was the biggest attraction, the most active of all, lived the longest and did the most."

Unlike Dicterow, some observers believe that first violinists are inclined to be Type A personalities and second violinists Type Bs. Whether that's true or not, "there's a different kind of virtuosity that goes into playing the inner, or lower, line," says Smiley. "It's challenging in a different way from the first violin part. Often you have to play in the middle or low register, where the instrument is not at its most brilliant. To bring out that middle register takes a different technique from the one you learn, generally speaking, as a violinist."

NO 'VIRTUOSOS'

One observation occurs more than any other from musicians who play second violin full time, and that's their sense of the music as a whole. A second violinist in a major American orchestra who preferred to remain anonymous put it this way: "The orchestra is not the place for virtuosity. In fact, often the 'virtuosos' can be the problem in certain musical situations. Blending is everything." And second violinists seem utterly attuned to the orchestra as a single entity and to their contribution to it.

"I think you have to subsume yourself into the whole," Smiley says. "When we have a long accompanying passage that's repetitive, that could become monotonous, I listen to whoever has the melody, and even though I may be playing off-beats, in my mind I'm playing the melody.

"It's a very thrilling feeling to feel wired into this mega, gigantic string organism. It's not always the most glamorous, but it's very heartfelt — it's the soul of music-making at that level," he says. "When you're playing the second violin part, you can see the textures, the almost brocade-like tapestry."

OTHER MUSICAL MUSINGS

THE MOM-CENTRIC METHOD

The popular and successful Suzuki system of teaching a child a musical instrument — begun by a Japanese violinist in the 1940s — takes a family commitment

September 07, 2003

GROWING up in South Korea, Connie Paik took music lessons for granted. "Every child learned the piano," she recalls. "It was a basic, just part of the curriculum: math, science, piano, etc. If your parents didn't start you on piano, then there was something wrong with your parents."

Paik, now a homemaker in Torrance, has observed that "many American mothers think music is something special, that they can only do it when the kid is 'talented' or 'gifted.' They don't think the same way about sports."

Not Paik. William, her 4-year-old, already studies piano. His sister, Erin, 6, is a violin student. They've both been studying for more than a year. Paik's far from being a stage mother, but she's not a soccer mom, either. She's a Suzuki mom. And that doesn't mean the kids are also riding choppers with training wheels.

The Paiks are part of a worldwide phenomenon — parents and children enrolled in the Suzuki method of learning a musical instrument. Developed in the 1940s by Japanese violinist Shinichi Suzuki and imported to the U.S. in the early '60s, this system of teaching the violin to kids as young as 2 has since been adapted to many other instruments and includes thousands of teachers and hundreds of thousands of pupils in 42 countries. Suzuki's goal wasn't to turn out concert artists. Nevertheless, Suzuki alumni include the hot young violinists Joshua Bell, Hillary Hahn and Leila Josefowicz, L.A. Philharmonic principal concertmaster Martin Chalifour, and Aimee Kreston, concertmaster of the Pasadena Symphony.

While studying violin in Germany during World War II, Suzuki had an epiphany: A baby in a German-speaking family who hears the frequent repetition of such basic words as "Mama" and "Dada," he realized, easily begins speaking German, whereas babies growing up in Japan learn Japanese. Suzuki reasoned that very young children introduced to the violin in the same way could just as naturally learn to play it — as long as they had the same loving and supportive environment.

Suzuki called this method the mother-tongue approach. He also determined that for the child to be exposed to repetitions equivalent to what a baby experiences with language, she must have more than once-a-week-lessons. He proposed a triangle — child, teacher and home teacher.

Says Anna Guenthner of Wood Ranch in Simi Valley, mother of 7-year-old violin student Brieana: "It's not about dropping off your child and going to get your groceries."

MOM'S ROLE USUALLY THE BIGGEST

For many parents, the Suzuki method, like Jell-O or Kleenex, is a respected brand name, which gives it a kind of authority. The surprise is that while sometimes the role of home teacher is played by a father or other caregiver, it usually goes to the mother, whether she has ever picked up a violin or not. In addition to playing recordings of the Suzuki repertoire, she must be well versed enough in violin playing to instruct her child.

Asked whether she knew what she was getting into when she signed up seven years ago with her 5-year-old twins, banking consultant Teri Zakzook of Santa Monica says: "Not at all. I took piano lessons when I was young, and my teacher used to step on my foot as an exclamation point."

Psychologist Laura Baker of Hancock Park — mother of Morgan Cesa, 14 (piano), Colin Cesa, 12 (violin), and Cameron Cesa, 10 (cello) — studied piano in her childhood and found her lessons "boring." Yet, she says, she got "hooked on the Suzuki method because I thought this is a really great way to start kids much younger, so they can get a lot further before they get to that point in their lives socially where they may decide they don't have enough time, and they can make those choices in a different way."

For Baker, discovering boys when she was 14 distracted her from continuing music lessons. Not so with Morgan, who entered 10th grade this fall and has studied piano since she was 5.

"She made the transition from being nagged to practice to being independent," Baker says. Moreover, her daughter doesn't do conventional baby-sitting. "She practices and does theory with six kids in the neighborhood."

Stacy Belanger of Van Nuys, whose 10-year-old, Christopher, started violin when he was 6, describes her task as "to make the time available so we can practice, to really pay attention at the lesson. I take copious notes. We tape the lessons. The tape reminds us of things. I can say: 'Remember she said she wants you to do this and this and this.'"

Given the ages of many Suzuki beginners, misunderstandings are inevitable. One mother found her child in the bathtub using a soapy washcloth on her violin. That afternoon, her teacher had instructed her to clean the instrument "every day, just the way you get cleaned every day."

Besides frequently hearing her mother play the pieces, the Suzuki student is required to listen daily to recordings of the music she will be playing. The idea is that she'll become so familiar with the Suzuki repertoire that she can sing it in her sleep and, once she has some technical facility, figure the pieces out on her instrument. Explains Beth Snowden-Ifft of Pasadena, an optometrist and mother of Susannah, 11 (violin), and Jim, 6 (violin): "They can then concentrate on technique and making music. They don't have to learn both the new instrument and the new skill of music reading at the same time."

On the basis that one wouldn't dream of teaching reading to a baby still learning to talk, Suzuki separated those tasks.

Belanger loves that "they go to bed singing, they wake up singing."

Teachers routinely recommend books by and about Suzuki; "Nurtured by Love," a video of the film based on his book of the same name; and other material that can bring a parent up to speed on not only the pedagogy but the philosophy of the method. Many teachers urge prospective parents to attend an orientation course. The Colburn School of Performing Arts requires incoming Suzuki parents to take its class.

Belanger appreciated the seven-week class given by the Suzuki Program of Los Angeles because it familiarized her with what her responsibilities were going to be.

"It taught us to be more patient, make allowances, be more cognizant of how learning happens, to figure out how to make it fun."

Does she ever lose her temper? Son Christopher is one of many kids who rolls his eyes at this question. After all, we're talking mothers and children here, not saints and angels.

Audie Mark of Burbank, who grew up in Guatemala, was determined to give her child what was unavailable to her then.

"Being a Suzuki mother is not easy. You have to be organized, flexible, on task," Mark says. "Every morning we wake up to the Suzuki music. It's my husband's job to push the button of the CD."

Mark was attracted to the Suzuki method because of what she read about its "training the ear." But practicing with 9-year-old Anthony day after day since he began at 4 has given her compassion for what he is trying to do: "It taught me it's not easy to hold the violin — and my motor skills are as developed as they're going to be."

When Shinichi Suzuki died in Tokyo in 1998 at age 99, Mark says, "I cried.... I felt that I knew him. I felt that it was a wonderful thing that he did for society, not just for children. All a parent wants is the best for their children, and this is the best."

For her part, Laura Baker says she "learned a lot about parenting through our music lessons. Teaching your children good habits and discipline is just something you need to do as a parent."

Some Suzuki moms find an extra mile they're willing to go for their offspring. Brieana Guenthner, who began violin two weeks before her third birthday, describes a difficult time when her mother, an educator, was teaching in a classroom by day and finishing her master's degree at night: "My mom was working too much. We couldn't have so much time to practice."

"So what did we do on the way to school?" Anna gently prods her daughter.

"Practice in the car," whispers Brieana, as if she's not supposed to tell anyone.

Anna laughs, remembering those days: "I was driving a little four-door ...." And Brieana played the violin wearing her seat belt?

"Of course."

FIVE-DAY MUSIC CAMPS

In addition to private lessons, group classes, master classes and recitals throughout the year, every summer there are more than 65 Suzuki Institutes (five-day music camps) across the United States alone. Most are held on college campuses. Each involves a few hundred campers — accompanied mostly by mothers.

The institutes are the high point of the Suzuki year. Late last spring, Anna Guenthner learned that a close friend of Brieana's from the previous two summers would be unable to attend this year's institute, so she asked her daughter if she still wanted to go.

The reply: "Mom, that's the reason I've been practicing every week!"

As it has for the past 15 years, the Southern California Suzuki Institute took place this summer at Occidental College in Eagle Rock. From July 20 through 25, the dorms were taken over by children of varying ages as well as many mothers. Some families chose to commute. For some, the event is their summer vacation. For Janis Simon of West Los Angeles, Suzuki camp began in June when she went with 10-year-old Mathew to the National Cello Institute, held in Claremont, and continued when she brought Elizabeth, 9, to the Occidental program for violinists.

There, the thrill felt by children surrounded by other kids playing instruments was palpable. In addition to violin, the Occidental Institute includes classes for cello, viola, guitar and flute. A different parent education class was offered daily. Despite the considerable heat, students practiced under the trees scattered across the verdant campus. Audiences for the daily 11 a.m. and evening concerts literally hummed as parents and children, from infants to teenagers, all soaked up music.

BENEFIT BEYOND THE EARLY YEARS?

Some professional musicians are disdainful of the Suzuki method. Soloist and teacher Stuart Canin, a onetime concertmaster of the San Francisco Symphony who's now concertmaster of Los Angeles Opera, says: "I've seen extraordinarily good work in the very early years. But if it goes on too long, it can be detrimental to the musical development of a gifted student."

But according to Robert Lipsett, who holds the Jascha Heifetz chair at the Colburn School and is an associate professor of violin at USC, "if you look at all the great violinists, they probably had a parent who was a violinist or a musician who practiced with them, and the results were spectacular. Suzuki figured out a way for everybody to do that. He proved that anyone could play the violin."

Lipsett adds: "Most of the 'players' coming up started with the Suzuki method. It's very good at making performing fun. If the teacher is sensitive, there's no reason why the student wouldn't develop well."

Is there room for abuse? Certainly. No doubt there are some parents who miss Suzuki's main objective — to build a beautiful character. But then again, there has always been room for abuse of children in the arts. The Suzuki method sets out a very simple plan. Anna Guenthner observes that some parents not involved with the method miss the point when they are simply stunned seeing a youngster play a very difficult piece.

"They say, 'Wow, this little child can really play,' and I'm thinking, 'You have to go beyond that. It's more than that! It's a way of life.'"

For Connie Paik, being a Suzuki mom is not such a big deal.

"If my kid wasn't doing so well in soccer," she says, "I would practice kicking the ball with her in the backyard. We do the same thing, except kicking the ball is a lot easier than playing the violin."

Returning from Germany to a Japan devastated by war, Suzuki wanted to give the children there something that would help them transcend hardships and unhappiness — to live a more rewarding life. Today, some parents probably encourage their children to take up an instrument in hopes that it will boost their math skills or, years down the road, their chances of gaining admission to a good college. But beyond that, perhaps they sense what a deeply moved Pablo Casals, the great cellist and friend of Suzuki, said in 1961 after hearing 400 Suzuki students perform: "It may very well be music which will save the world."

IRMA NEUMANN: FIDDLING HER WAY THROUGH HISTORY

For almost 60 years, studio musician Irma Neumann has fiddled while Rome burned and the Titanic sank — twice
November 09, 2003

EVEN if you sit through the end credits of a movie, watching the crawl that lists all the little people who belong to unions requiring that their contributions be acknowledged, you're still not seeing the names of a host of anonymous laborers in the filmmaking process. If a picture has a big symphonic score, the credits may be missing as many as a hundred musicians.

Violinist Irma Neumann, a white-haired, jolly-looking woman who will be 88 on her next birthday, is one such player. She has worked on countless films, TV shows and commercials.

Neumann began participating in scoring sessions nearly 60 years ago. In 1953, she played for *Titanic* under composer Sol Kaplan and in 1997 for *Titanic*," scored by James Horner. She has played for Alex North, Bernard Herrmann, Dmitri Tiomkin, Henry Mancini and Randy Newman, on films ranging from *Butch Cassidy and the Sundance Kid* to *M*A*S*H* to *Cleopatra*. Her recent credits include the *The Matrix Revolutions*, the coming HBO adaptation of *Angels in America* and the soon-to-be-released *The Cat in the Hat*.

And she has no intention of retiring.

When she goes to work these days, Neumann says, "it's different, because I don't know a lot of the people. Everybody looks so young. I stick out. I'm greeted as if I were something special." But, she says, "I don't know what I'd do if I didn't play the fiddle."

Neumann grew up in Los Angeles. Her mother was a painter who dabbled on the violin; her older sister, Pauline, now 92, studied piano. By the time she was 5, Irma was determined that she too would play the violin.

"Wouldn't you rather have a cello?" her mother asked. No. There was always a violin in the house. And lest you get the wrong impression, she adds, "I didn't fool with it."

By her mid-20s, however, she had studied with several teachers and become proficient enough to play in orchestras and as a soloist for both local and national radio broadcasts. "I had no dreams of playing in the studios," she says. "I had a trio with Pauline and a cellist named Louise Friedhofer. Louise's brother was a composer for the movies, Hugo Friedhofer" — whose best-known score was to be *The Best Years of Our Lives* in 1946.

In 1943, Neumann auditioned for and joined the Los Angeles Philharmonic. But in those days, movie studios had their own orchestras — there were eight at the time, she recalls — and two years later, she was offered a job playing at 20th Century Fox. She decided to go for it.

The year Neumann joined the Fox orchestra, 1946, the music department was headed by composer-conductor Alfred Newman and his brothers, Lionel and Emil. There were only six women in the orchestra: a harpist, a flutist, a violist, a cellist, another violinist and Neumann. Occasionally, she remembers, the flute player had trouble breathing. "The room was blue. Everybody smoked. People carved out notches on the wooden stands to put their lit cigarettes. While we were playing, the cigarettes were still lit."

Fox orchestra members signed a contract every year. "We were paid 10 hours a week whether we worked or not. We were paid two weeks' double pay for vacation. We never did 10 hours a week all the years I was there. Some studios did. The contracts lasted for 10 years, and then the producers decided they were spending too much, so it was done away with and we were just paid by the hour, as we are now."

Being a freelance musician, Neumann has played on numerous recordings as well. She was in the Roger Wagner Chorale for 15 years and played 31 seasons with the Glendale Symphony. She soloed with the Pasadena Symphony, playing a Paganini concerto.

"I've played the Academy Awards 28 times. The first time I played it was when Lionel [Newman] was invited to do it. Lionel insisted on using his own orchestra," the Fox ensemble.

Neumann regrets that the format of scoring has changed. It was more interesting in the old days, she says, when "you felt as if you were a real part of it." Until just a few years ago, the orchestra sat in a semicircle facing the conductor, who could watch the musicians as well as an enormous screen showing the movie behind the orchestra. Special streamers were placed on the film to indicate when the music should begin and end. Musicians heard what they had done on a playback in the orchestra room. Sometimes the orchestra even heard the dialogue track, and some composer-conductors even gave the members a little synopsis of the film, not for "Method" playing but just to be kind, informative or chatty in a business with serious money and time constraints.

She is sorry that nowadays there is no giant screen. Musicians play on films with no knowledge of the plot, the actors or any of the particulars. The conductor still has his timing streamers, but they are on the screen of a small video monitor next to him.

On the other hand, there are now far more female players than in 1946, though not as many as men. The base pay is about $500 for a six-hour session, and there are also health and welfare benefits and residuals.

Neumann is not a sentimental dame. Yet there is a touch of something in her voice when she talks about playing for the Newman brothers, David and Tom, sons of Alfred, nephews of Lionel and Emil and cousins of Randy. She recounts bumping into Tom and his wife at a book signing for a memoir by Louis Kaufman, a former concertmaster at Fox, that was completed by his widow, Annette. According to Neumann, "Tommy said, 'Somebody told me you had quit playing.' I said no. 'Oh, I'll see you,' he said."

A few weeks later, Newman, standing on the podium conducting his score for *Angels in America*, broke into a big smile when he spotted Neumann in the violin section, her singular snowy head of hair sparkling in a sea of blond and dark hues.

"Hi, Irma!" he said, and waved.

BEYOND THE BRASS BANDS

Among the U.S. military's scores of musical ensembles are top string players who can spend their entire careers based in the nation's capital
October 23, 2005

IN October 1944, Stuart Canin was an 18-year-old violinist bound for Juilliard. Then he was drafted. His basic training was even cut short by four weeks, so that he and other new recruits could get to Europe as quickly as possible.

"I carried my rifle and a fiddle," recalls Canin, concertmaster of the Los Angeles Opera. "I still remember the guy watching me walk across the gangplank who asked, 'What are you going to do with that?' I said, 'You never know.'"

True enough. By July 1945, two months after V-E Day, Canin found himself a member of the 6817th Soldiers Show Company, touring hospitals on the Continent with the likes of Mickey Rooney, Joshua Logan, pianist Eugene List "and a whole bunch of fiddle players."

Soon after, Canin and List "were informed that President

Truman was coming to Europe for a conference, so we were pulled from the company and flown to Berlin and driven to a suburb in order to provide some of the entertainment for a dinner Truman was giving."

Canin and List watched as "one big black limousine after another rolled up. We recognized Truman, Marshal Stalin wearing his khaki uniform with the shoulder board, and Churchill smoking a cigar, Adm. Leahy, Gen. Marshall, Secretary of State Byrnes, Molotov — the whole cast of characters on the front page of the New York Times if you read it for a week."

Canin still has the V-Mail he sent his parents the next day from the site: Potsdam.

Afterward, the Army "sent Gene and me to Army camps to see if we could cull bassoon players, oboe players, instrumentalists still in Europe who had played professionally. In September, our whole unit was transferred to Frankfurt, Germany. By that time, they had enough players to make up the first symphony organized for the Army, which they called the GI Symphony. It was later superseded by the 7th Army Symphony. We gave concerts for GIs, British, Russian and French troops, traveling in ambulances, about eight to an ambulance — which were damn cold in the winter."

As the occupation of Iraq wears on, prompting criticism of its human and financial costs, there's one item in the Pentagon budget that is rarely remarked upon: musicians in uniform. Although people hear brass bands marching up and down parade grounds, comparatively few members of the public have an opportunity to hear military string players — top-notch, conservatory-trained musicians who can spend their entire military careers based in the nation's capital.

And like Canin, who cofounded the San Francisco-based New Century Chamber Orchestra and is a former concertmaster of the San Francisco Symphony, many from these ranks also go on to fruitful civilian careers.

The U.S. military has more than 150 service bands all over the world — 8,000 to 10,000 musicians total, if all slots were filled. There are even bands in Afghanistan and Iraq. Each service — Army, Air Force, Marines, Navy and Coast Guard, which is part of Homeland Security — has its own bands and music budgets. In 2006, for example, the Navy alone will spend more than $2 million on its Washington band and 12 fleet bands, the Defense Department says.

Many military musicians have a secondary duty and are trained should they need to fight. But there are also five first-rank "premier" service bands based in the Washington, D.C., area: the Navy Band, the Army Field Band and three bands that include strings — the Army's "Pershing's Own," the Marines' "The President's Own" and the Air Force Band. (After a 1960 plane crash over Rio de Janeiro took the lives of 18 Navy string players, the Navy Band never rebuilt its string section.) The string sections each perform alone — typically show music and light classics — but players also mingle with other musicians to form symphony orchestras, chamber ensembles and smaller groups.

All three string sections play at the White House and State Department, but members of "The President's Own" don't go through boot camp, says Gunnery Sgt. Kristin Mergen, its public affairs chief, "because we have one mission only: to perform for the president of the United States."

According to Lt. Cmdr. Lisa Brackenbury at the Pentagon Navy news desk, " 'The President's Own' was founded on July 11, 1798, and is considered the oldest musical organization in America."

AN ALTERNATIVE TO STUDENT DEFERMENT

In 1965, as the Vietnam War was intensifying, Alan de Veritch, a viola protege of William Primrose at Indiana University, was already concertizing. As a result, he says, "I was not able to maintain the minimum number of required courses to be classified as a full-time student. It was just a matter of time before I was going to lose my student deferment."

De Veritch's father, a violinist, was anxious to find a way to sustain his son's concert career, so he researched opportunities for musicians in the military. He discovered that musicians in "post bands or fort bands were part of the regular fort, so if that fort gets shipped out to fight the battle, even though you're a musician, you go and you fight."

De Veritch's father also found out about "all these different musical entities that were centered in Washington, D.C., and discovered that the Marine Band did carry strings." So De Veritch enlisted and joined the Marine Band, knowing he was signing on for White House duty.

Daniel Rothmuller, a cellist with the Los Angeles Philharmonic for the last 35 years and associate principal since 1975, was in a string quartet with De Veritch at Indiana. Rothmuller recalls, "My number was up. I had already had my Army physical." It was De Veritch "who talked me into auditioning for the service bands. I was offered West Point in a piano trio or the White House Orchestra, basically a dinner orchestra."

Rothmuller, who took the White House option, remembers the unique stress of the audition: "In this case, you were auditioning literally for your life."

Violinist Raymond Kobler was at Indiana at the same time. A former associate concertmaster of the Cleveland Orchestra and former concertmaster of the San Francisco Symphony, today he's concertmaster of the Pacific Symphony and a busy freelancer. Looking back 40 years, he says, "Danny and I enlisted together, took the oath in Indianapolis signing away four years of our lives to the Marine Corps. We went in as college students, came out in an absolute daze as instant staff sergeants and promptly got two jaywalking tickets.

"We arrived in Washington on Jan. 31, 1967. Friends laughed when they saw me: 'Look at that hair!' I had a huge Afro. 'It'll be gone tomorrow.' Who would have dreamed that within a week and a half, we'd be playing a state dinner in the White House for King Hassan of Morocco?"

De Veritch says, "I went to the powers that be at the Marine Band and negotiated that Danny, Ray and violinist Andrew Zaplatinsky would join me there, and we would be called the White House String Quartet, an unofficial unit of the Marine Band. They gave us about two days of the basics so we wouldn't look like total idiots. 'This is how you tell who's an officer. This is how you salute, shine your shoes, how to polish the brass on your uniform.' But even then, we did look like idiots half the time."

Rothmuller remembers the officer in charge of the Marine Strings, Col. Albert Schopper, telling them, "Dean Rusk is throwing the Jefferson Day dinner for Bruno Kreisky, the Austrian chancellor. You boys know any quartets written around the time of Thomas Jefferson?" "Yes, sir, we do," Rothmuller remembers saying, while "trying to keep a straight face and stand at attention. So we decided to sight-read Haydn's Emperor Quartet, which has the Austrian national anthem in it.

"We started playing, everyone's talking, when suddenly the chancellor hits his glass and is shushing everybody. Nobody could move. We had been having a good time. All of a sudden, they're staring at us, listening to every note."

Kobler remembers the fear they felt as "we shifted gears and were now playing a concert. And you get nervous, you start sweating, going into concert mode. We had to stop playing after 20 minutes because nobody could eat or talk."

Rothmuller laughs as he recalls the aftereffects: "Our stock went way up at the State Department. ... The next time the quartet showed up, we were served dinner, like the grown-ups."

During their stint as the White House String Quartet, the men were also frequent guests at Justice Abe Fortas' house for dinner and chamber music. Fortas, an amateur violinist, had made it clear to President Lyndon Johnson that he was not to be disturbed on Sunday nights, when he played chamber music with friends.

De Veritch remembers: "You'd sit around the dinner table with three or four other justices of the Supreme Court and maybe Henry Kissinger, just key people. There would be some political talk, but nothing confidential." He added that when Fortas resigned in May 1969, newspapers printed a photograph showing Rothmuller, Budapest String Quartet violinist Alexander Schneider, "Abe Fortas and me playing quartets in the foyer of the White House. And behind us are LBJ, George Meany, Gerald Ford and the rest of the Marine Strings, all watching us."

After the members of the White House String Quartet finished serving their four years, they still faced two years in the reserves. De Veritch figured "they probably weren't going to call the people who were least qualified, which was us." But, toying with the idea of continuing to perform under the name "White House Quartet," he wrote to President Richard Nixon. Five days before the Watergate scandal broke, he received a letter from the White House counsel declining authorization of the name. De Veritch still has the letter, written and signed by John Dean III.

ANOTHER CAREER PATH FOR MUSICIANS

Now on the faculty at Indiana University, De Veritch says, "As far back as I can remember, brass players, percussionists and winds always looked at openings in the military bands as a viable option to symphonies. In recent years, a lot of the string players do as well. All of my students contemplating orchestra careers, taking auditions, also look into the military bands."

Rothmuller delineates the perks: "You have everything taken care of — retirement, medical, PX, which is the military store. They sell every single thing you can imagine. And it's like buying wholesale. So you might not be making as much money as you would with the New York Philharmonic or the National Symphony, but then again, you don't have to spend that money. It's security. You can't get more security than what the armed forces gives you."

The biggest difference in service bands today, versus the Vietnam era, is that women are included. In 1995, violinist Dionisia Fernandez, a Juilliard graduate, was freelancing in Washington, D.C., when string player friends in the Army Band told her about an opening. She remembers thinking, "That's weird. Army strings?" But "it just opened up a whole new world of musicians for me here. A lot of musicians don't know about that."

The Army Band, like the Air Force Band, requires basic training of its musicians. Fernandez was 29 when she went to boot camp, training with 18- and 19-year-olds. Today she's a sergeant first class, one of the 18 string players and one accordion player who make up "Pershing's Own," performing at dinners at the White House and State Department and for various military functions.

Although the Marine Band strings perform during cocktails and the main course and again after dessert, the Army or Air Force strings play everything from memory and "come out strolling during dessert," she says.

De Veritch explains that the "strolling strings" are "more like a featured entertainer."

Army Strings, Fernandez says, is a wonderful job for a mom with kids: "I'm there four days a week but not gone all day, which is perfect. Right now, we have a few expectant moms in maternity uniforms when they stroll."

Fernandez explains that even though the Marine Band skips basic training, "they still have to weigh in." She adds, "There's no flexibility. It's as strict as training to be on the front line." Band members are required to do a physical fitness test "and have to do our two-mile run every six months. The logic is, we may be musicians, but when we play for generals, we're soldiers in the U.S. military."

With the shortage of troops in Iraq and the redeployment of others, there's been speculation about reinstatement of the draft. Were that to happen, there would likely be even more competition for positions in military bands. As it is, there already are many more professionally trained musicians in the U.S. than orchestral jobs. The August issue of the journal International Musician listed two vacancies in the Air Force Strings: one for violin, the other for cello. In the September issue, they were gone.

Kobler says, "We were very lucky to be able to fulfill our military obligation and not have a disruption in our careers, as so many did. We were extremely grateful."

He remembers a former roommate, violist Phil Eastham, who wasn't so lucky: "Phil was the sweetest guy, the last person you would think of carrying a rifle or anything. He is on the wall of the Vietnam Memorial."

PIANO TECHNICIANS: PULLING STRINGS TO GET IT RIGHT

When the stakes are high but the instrument's an unknown, many pianists insist on the technician they trust to put a performance in its best light

September 03, 2006

UNTIL just recently, a violin soloist took for granted that she could carry her fiddle with her on an airplane. A concert cellist was able to buy a seat for his instrument whenever he flew. But even before heightened airline security, concert pianists were not so lucky: Almost all of them must leave their humongous, beloved instrument at home and make do with one they've quite likely never played before.

To ease their discomfort, however, these musicians have an indispensable ally, the unsung hero or heroine of many a concert and recital — the piano technician. That's the person at each venue who prepares the piano in every respect, doing whatever possible to make a soloist feel at home when he or she sits down to perform. Ron Elliott is going into his 20th year as the Los Angeles Philharmonic's piano technician, handling all nine of its Steinway concert pianos at the Hollywood Bowl and Walt Disney Concert Hall. And as he puts it: "I am on standby for all soloists until they're finished."

Obviously, we're talking here about more than your garden-variety piano tuner. Piano technician Gordon McNelly is retail service manager at Steinway & Sons in New York, where he oversees 12 other technicians. And according to McNelly, a piano tuner "just tunes. He doesn't get into the subtleties, adjusting little nuances of making that piano what the instrumentalist needs." Gerhard Feldmann, president of Bösendorfer New York, the only exclusive showroom for Bösendorfer pianos outside Vienna, likens a tuner to someone in the car business who "works at Jiffy Lube and just knows how to change the oil — as opposed to a Mercedes-Benz technician, who knows how to maintain and service the entire vehicle."

To most people, in other words, the piano may be just a parlor instrument. But, says Elliott, a concert pianist is like "a race car driver who takes it around that track, and his life depends on it. It has to be able to perform."

MULTIPRONGED APPROACH

In fact, as Elliott explains, there are three distinct steps in piano care that come before tuning, which consists basically of adjusting the tension in the instrument's 200-plus strings so they vibrate with the correct frequency, or pitch. He calls that "the icing on the cake."

The first step involves the piano's "action." "The instrument consists of a box that has wood, steel and strings strung on it," Elliott says, "and the action, which slides out of the piano like a big drawer with perhaps 4,500 moving parts in it. The action is everything in between pressing the key down and the sound coming out of the instrument. I have to assess what has to be done to get that end product tone." McNelly likens the action, which determines how hard the hammers hit the strings, to "the engine of the instrument. That key, when you push it down, has to have a specified amount of resistance. It can't be too much or too little."

The next phase of maintaining a healthy piano is tone regulation, when the technician "goes through the piano chromatically to make sure that every note sounds even, that one is not sticking out more than any other," McNelly says. And finally, there is voicing — setting the instrument's tone, usually by modifying the hammers or the felt that covers them. When Feldmann prepares a piano for an artist, his first question is, "What is the program? Brahms? Debussy? Both?" "You can't voice the piano for every piece," he says, "but if I know what is being played and who is playing, I have a rough idea. You want to see how they attack, how they hold their fingers, to get an idea how to work on the instrument for them." McNelly adds: "Every instrument has its own voice. The ability to change that speaking voice falls to the piano technician. If the piano is used for accompaniment, you don't want it to overpower, be too harsh or too bright, so voicing would be the process of backing it off, making it a little more mellow."

Each of these steps demands intuition, experience and technical expertise, whereas many piano tuners nowadays rely on digital tuning devices. But on that subject, McNelly is unequivocal. "I don't employ technicians who use them," he says. "Besides tuning, you're listening for clicks, things that need to be fixed. Relying visually on a digital device does not allow your ears to pick up the nuances of this acoustic instrument. Once you set that piece of electronic equipment on top of the piano, you lose credibility."

Elliott remembers working in New York in the '80s and frequently going to Carnegie Hall "10 minutes before a performance — the audience is seated and the piano sounds terrible. It's survival. You can only rely on your brain and your ear. You have to go through it as quickly as possible, bring the thing together to be usable. And it's not possible with a machine. Every piano's not the same. To make it sound beautiful and resonant, you don't take the same approach."

"The sad truth," says McNelly, "is that the industry is horribly unregulated. Anyone can open a business and work on pianos. There's no licensing, no certification, no union, no anything. You don't even need to be insured. Even the used car business has regulations now. I don't know of any other industry like this. Maybe bowling ball drillers. It's pretty bad."

A PASSION FOR THE PIANO

Henry Steinway, 91, great-grandson of the founder of Steinway & Sons, still goes to work most days at the firm's West 57th Street headquarters in Manhattan. Seated behind his desk one afternoon last spring, he observed that piano technicians are "very interesting people." Standing amid her vast collection of music boxes with her two Pyrenees mountain dogs nearby, Tali Mahanor, considered one of the New York area's finest piano technicians, puts it somewhat differently. "We're a weird and odd lot," she says with a laugh.

Today, Mahanor has her own business, called Cantabile Piano Arts, in Yonkers, N.Y. But she says she was "around 12 when I acquired my first piano, for $25 — it had one ivory on the keyboard" — and she recalls the first time it was tuned as a well-nigh transcendent experience. There was "a purity, a beauty in that gorgeous clear sound of a tuned piano. I was in tears pretty much that day. But of course it eventually started losing that beauty, like windows that become dirty again."

Mahanor's parents couldn't hear the difference, though, and refused to pay to have the instrument retuned, "so I took a wrench and deliberately put it way out of tune." After that, "I don't know how she found it, but my mother actually bought me a home study course from the American School of Piano Tuning, which is now online. There were 10 lessons and a little test at the end of each one. I was in seventh grade when I made the decision that this was what I wanted to do. By the time I reached high school, I had piano tunings every day after school."

When she was a junior, Mahanor went to Steinway & Sons in New York to talk about job opportunities. "I passed the tuning audition," she says, "and it was arranged that I would work there when I completed a one-year program in Sioux City, Iowa, which I wanted to attend. It closed up a few years ago. It was a dying art back then."

Elliott, for his part, started out to be a pianist before learning the craft of tuning and taking a job in the concert department at Steinway in New York. After several years, he came west and ran the Steinway concert/artist department at Sherman Clay in Los Angeles for a short time, then went to work for the Philharmonic. But even he acknowledges that to be a first-rate piano technician, you need something beyond the physical and aural skills. You need an understanding of emotional fragility.

"One of the things about doing standby — it's not just in case something happens," he says. Pianists "feel more confident if I'm there. A lot of it is psychological." Feldmann agrees, noting that "sometimes these artists, who go all over the world, like to see a familiar face. The piano may have been neglected, but when they know that you're coming, they know that you will do whatever it takes to make this thing play well and make their work easier."

Feldmann says he enjoys being at concerts but also finds them "nerve-racking, because you're always listening. Did something slip or is something going out of tune? The greatest concert is when someone plays a heavy two-hour program and at the end you still don't hear any out-of-tune notes on the piano. That's the ultimate as a piano technician."

Certainly the prospect of fame is not a motivator for these dedicated individuals. Yet they sometimes receive their due. "Years ago," Elliott recalls, "during a televised concert of a piano concerto at the Bowl, a string broke, hit the inside of the lid, rattled the strings, fell on the sound board and continued to rattle."

The conductor signaled him, and the broadcast announcer gave a blow-by-blow description: " 'Here comes Ron Elliott....' I looked in and pulled the string out." Then, his accustomed anonymity gone, Elliott was astounded to find 18,000 people applauding. "The pianist got up, shook my hand and bowed."

CAPTURING A SOUND THAT RINGS TRUE

Immortalizing a performance takes more than hanging a mic and hitting 'record.' There's an art to these engineers' science.
Dec. 2, 2007

THE average pop music fan, if asked, could probably come up with at least a handful of names of notable record producers. Rick Rubin, George Martin, Timbaland, Brian Eno, Phil Spector are all well known. It seems fair to say, though, that the typical consumer of orchestral and chamber music recordings, faced with the same question, would draw a blank.

Yet as much as in rock 'n' roll or hip-hop, the engineer for such music, who is often, though not always, the producer as well, is the person who makes or breaks an audio performance. He chooses and then places the microphones for a recording session and later meticulously splices various takes, in the old days with a razor blade and tape, today on a computer, to achieve the best possible version of a composition. It's a version that may well reach far more listeners than the work being played did for many years after its premiere.

Indeed, Max Wilcox, 78, who has won five Grammys and whose recordings have garnered 17, speaks for the majority of his peers when he insists that his job is primarily musical: "I'm not a techie," he says. As a producer, Wilcox consults the musical score while supervising a recording, and he brings to his task not only his background as a classical pianist but also some experience as a conductor. "I have to be enough of an audience to play for, not that I'm so important," he says. The point, rather, is that the musicians being recorded are assured that "their musical output is being monitored and evaluated, both by them during playbacks and by me."

"Artur Rubinstein never chose a take in his life with me," Wilcox recalls of his working relationship with the famed pianist. "But we were so closely allied in our musical feelings that I could tell pretty much from the recording session what he liked better, and since we wound up making about 60 LPs together, we were something like musical twins. He referred to me as his collaborator, not his producer."

Recording engineer-producers often start out as electronic fiddlers, tinkerers. Take Chinese-born, New York-based Da-Hong Seetoo, 47, who is engineer and producer for the Tokyo and Emerson string quartets as well as many other ensembles. Seetoo was 6, living in Shanghai, when China's Cultural Revolution began and the record collection and huge sheet music library of his father, principal second violinist of the Shanghai Symphony, were confiscated. Under cover of darkness, blinds drawn, windows closed, the elder man taught violin to Da-Hong and his two siblings. The family also listened to "escaped" LPs that circulated within the local musical community.

Then, one day, Seetoo's father brought home a "used Telefunken reel-to-reel tape machine, so we could listen to the recordings again and again." The thing was, he explains, "If you own an illegal machine gun and there's something wrong with it, you can't have someone else fix it." And thus was a technician born. Over time, and out of necessity, Seetoo "would take things apart and try to reverse-engineer them," repairing belts, bushings, microphones, amplifiers, speakers.

In 1977, at the end of the Cultural Revolution, he came to the U.S. to study violin and then began pursuing a career as a professional musician. Occasionally, he says, he would take an engineering job, "to help out friends." But suddenly, an "opportunity landed on me. Eugene Drucker," one of the two violinists in the Emerson String Quartet, "was in the middle of completing the Bach solo sonatas and partitas when the engineer fell ill, so he asked me if I could help him. I was playing, but I needed to make a living. And this stuff enables me to make a good living."

Armin Steiner might say the same thing. Steiner, 73, works chiefly on film and television scores, but he is widely regarded as among the past masters of engineering orchestral recordings. A native Angeleno, Steiner was the son of a concert pianist mother and a Hungarian international chess master father whose friends included many of the superstar classical music emigrés living in L.A. in the years before World War II. As a hobby, he recalls, his father recorded "Hungarian gypsy music in our house, direct to disk."

Young Armin's keen ear was nurtured by the violin, which he began studying while still a toddler. "Sound was of prime importance," he says. "How it projected." At the same time, at home he was acquiring technical know-how about recording, and inspired by his father's friend Michael Rettinger, an acoustician and a leading engineer at RCA, he went on to study acoustics at UCLA.

Like Seetoo, Steiner became a professional violinist. But after several years of freelancing in New York and touring as concertmaster of the Ballet Russe de Monte Carlo, he realized that "I didn't like this whole business of living out of a suitcase." That, combined with the sudden death of his father, caused him to want to try something else, and so, with the help of an uncle, he built a recording studio "in my father's chess club, over our garage on 108 N. Formosa."

For Steiner, "music was a wonderful foundation and the engineering was academic. I wanted to put these two things together." Over the next 20 years, even after he was forced to give up his home studio, he worked with Herb Alpert, Glen Campbell and numerous Motown artists, among many others. Then, in 1980, he received an offer from 20th Century Fox to record some classical music with the Los Angeles Philharmonic to be used on the soundtrack of television's *M*A*S*H*. He still remembers the "menu" for that first date: "Tchaikovsky Sixth, Tchaikovsky *Romeo and Juliet* and Stravinsky's *Firebird*. John Williams and Lionel Newman conducted. It started a wonderful romance with that stage. I probably did over 5,000 sessions between 1980 and 1992."

Like Wilcox, Steiner says he has "always considered myself a musician, even though I sit on the other side of the glass. We don't create anything. We are translators, translating what the composer put on paper, what we hear as a result. I think that when you feel that you are bigger than the music, you get yourself in big trouble."

So what, exactly, are the challenges facing this special fraternity? Fred Vogler, 43, is chief audio engineer for the Los Angeles Philharmonic, Los Angeles Opera and summer events at the Hollywood Bowl, as well as the occasional film score. He earned a degree in recording arts at USC and later interned at KUSC, and, he says, "Learning how to set up the equipment and everything that's associated with recording takes a lot of experience to do right. It's no different from having a guitar and handing it to different people. Some people are going to sound fantastic and some pretty lousy."

Lately, Vogler has been devoting a lot of his energy to recording Philharmonic concerts to be broadcast on the radio and made available for downloading via iTunes. For both, he says, he uses the orchestra's "main microphone system that captures most of the sound, and 'spot' mics, little area mics, that give a little more presence to the harp or the woodwind section, or if there's a piano upstage that sounds a little distant, we might enhance its sound. We record the three weekend performances, and then in conjunction with the assistant or associate conductor we'll mix and match and put together the best performance."

For Steiner as well, "It's not necessarily the microphone that's in front of the section that is the important microphone picking up the sound. It may be the microphone that's 50 feet away. I hear many recordings that are a collection of microphones rather than the sound of an orchestra. The orchestra is not what you hear from left to right, it's what you hear from front to back. It's the depth, the three-dimensionality, that gives the sound of an orchestra. Of course, those of us who have been in an orchestra have a better idea of what this should be. I approach my engineering from the player's viewpoint."

Steiner laments that today, "Many engineers record all the sections of the orchestra independently, in isolation, in a booth, or in a section separated by dividers. But then you don't have the relationships sonically that you have when people are all playing at the same time. It's not a very musical approach."

Perhaps unsurprisingly, Seetoo considers chamber music the most difficult to record. Unlike the experience of attending a performance, where generally even a front-row seat is at least 20 feet from the musicians, preserving such a performance for posterity, he says, involves microphones "two to three feet away from them. It's immediate. It's a 'full spectrum' sort of music, polyphonic, because you have multiple voices going at the same time. You can't hide with chamber music. With orchestra, if someone in the back of the second violin section plays a wrong note, you can't hear the difference."

The engineer, of course, can always combine different takes. Steiner, for example, remembers being hired in 1956 to edit the Bach unaccompanied violin sonatas and partitas for Hungarian violinist Joseph Szigeti, who was living in Palos Verdes. "When Szigeti recorded them, they just let the machines run," he says. "So, if he wanted to record the first 10 bars or the first eight bars or the first bar of the C-major Fugue or whatever, he would do it 10 or 15 times or more. So, they had all these bits and pieces. There were at least 100 reels of 1/4-inch tape. I spent three or four months editing those for him."

But according to Seetoo, "Postproduction is essentially a cut and paste job. If I didn't gather the material to begin with, I can't do anything at the end."

Wilcox agrees. "While you can eliminate mechanical imperfections, you can't make someone an artist by making 400 splices," he says. "You can't give a violinist a more beautiful tone or a better conception of the music or a better idea of the tempo. You can make it sound mechanically and technically solid, but all the things that make 'music' can't be fabricated."

That insight may help explain why Seetoo likens his job to being in the Secret Service. "I see and hear a lot," he says. "I know exactly how good or how bad one can play." For Wilcox too, the bond that the engineer-producer develops with artists is intensely personal: "You're dealing with the heart and soul of these people. You're their personal/musical physician/psychiatrist/cheerleader/

best friend/advisor." Wilcox, for example, has been pianist Richard Goode's recording producer for more than 30 years.

Engineers do have their tricks. Seetoo recalls how a few years ago, he recorded the Emersons playing the Mendelssohn *Octet for Strings*, with each of them doing the work of two instruments. That meant seating them in one configuration for a first "pass" and in another arrangement, wearing headphones to hear what they had already played, for a second run-through. The CD set containing the result, which he likens to a jigsaw puzzle, went on to win two Grammys, including one for his engineering.

Sometimes, though, sheer serendipity can account for at least part of a recording's power. Vogler, for instance, recalls recording Paul Salamunovich conducting the Los Angeles Master Chorale in 1997 in *Lux Aeterna*, by its then composer in residence, Morten Lauridsen.

"We were recording at Loyola Marymount Chapel, up on the hill, during one of the heaviest rains and wettest winters we've ever had in Southern California," Vogler says. "There was a full orchestra, full choir sessions all set up, and we had to somehow overcome the sound of the downpour outside and in the hallways."

They wound up using mats to muffle that sound, and "it made the sessions kind of magical," he says. "If you listen to quiet passages in the piece, you can hear the rain. It added something to the recording, played a part in the *Lux Aeterna*, the 'eternal light.'"

Leopold Auer

Abram Shtern

AUER TO HEIFETZ

At age 89, master violinist Abram Shtern keeps his impressive musical lineage going through a host of adoring students
November 02, 2008

APART from a select group of musicians, few people have heard of the violinist Abram Shtern. Unlike the late Jascha Heifetz, say, he has never felt obliged to travel incognito to avoid being recognized. Yet in July, "Abram Shtern Day" was declared during the first Montecito Summer Music Festival, and 112 students from 11 countries, along with an impressive faculty lineup, were on hand to help celebrate it. The reason is that Shtern, who will turn 90 in March, is not simply a musician. He is a revered teacher, a direct pedagogical descendant of Leopold Auer, the same man who taught Heifetz.

The world is jampacked with violin teachers. But there was only one Auer, a Hungarian who in 1868 signed a three-year contract at Russia's St. Petersburg Conservatory and then went on to exceed that contract by 46 years before coming to the U.S. in 1917. Besides Heifetz, a partial list of the astonishing roster of his proteges, sometimes known as the "Auer Gang," includes Mischa Elman, Tosha Seidel, Efrem Zimbalist and Nathan Milstein. So influential was Auer that in the 1920s, George and Ira Gershwin wrote a song, "Mischa, Yascha, Toscha, Sascha," that contains the lines

When we began our notes were very sour –

Until a man, Professor Auer,

Set out to show us, one and all,

How we could pack them in, in Carnegie Hall.

Great violin teachers, like great racehorses, frequently boast a distinguished lineage, and Auer was no exception. He had been a student of the Hungarian violinist Joseph Joachim, a mentor and muse of Brahms, Dvorak, Bruch and Schumann.

Which brings us back to Shtern: Born in 1918 in Kiev, in what is now Ukraine, and an L.A. resident since 1990, he studied with David Berthier, who in turn had studied with Auer. Shtern is a frail man today. He speaks little English. But the portrait of him that emerges from conversations with violinists he has coached is of the ideal teacher: not only a professional instructor but a life inspiration.

'LAST OF MOHICANS'

Reminiscing via his daughter, Ludmila Shtern, Shtern said recently that his inauspicious violin roots began with his pummeling a klezmer player, a Jewish folk violinist who had come to the Shtern household to instruct little Abram. Shtern, it was observed, had a very fine ear and a sensibility to match. Luckily, the klezmer player took a hint. But on his way out, he noted that Shtern had talent and recommended violin lessons.

Eventually, Shtern became assistant to Berthier at the Kiev

Conservatory. As concertmaster of the Shevchenko Opera and Ballet Orchestra from 1947 to 1989, he was also a frequent soloist and chamber musician. According to his former student Alexander Kirillov, a New York violinist, Shtern was "the best musician and violinist, not just in our area. He was kind of the last of the Mohicans."

Kirillov, 52, knew about Shtern long before he had the courage to play for him at age 19. Until then, he recalls, "I played guitar in a band, football, pretty much everything except practicing. He didn't push me. He just told me how it might be and showed me some different way in this life. So when I left his house that day, after three hours, I was a completely different person."

Another former Shtern student, Igor Polesitsky, 50, principal violist of the Maggio Musicale Orchestra in Florence, Italy, describes his mentor as "kind of a natural genius of the violin, who could play violin lying down on the floor or sitting in an armchair."

Kiev is 68 miles south of Chernobyl, the site in 1986 of the worst nuclear power plant disaster in history, whose fallout was far greater than that released in the bombings of Hiroshima and Nagasaki. Afterward, according to Kirillov, "it was an absolutely forbidden subject. Everything was hidden from people. Even now, nobody knows the whole truth. All I can say is it was extremely bad, especially for children." The Shtern family, his daughter said, decided to immigrate to the United States and was finally able to do so in 1989.

Elizabeth Wilson, 48, a freelance violinist and violist who frequently subs with the Los Angeles Philharmonic, explains that at the time, "Russian Jews leaving Russia, depending on whether they were going to Israel or the States, had to stay in some kind of holding station. The ones going to the States stayed just outside Rome for about three months, until their visas were in order, and that's when I was living in Italy." Wilson was staying in a Russian household, and "we had a lot of Russian guests coming through. Abram was one of them." He even taught some master classes, "and so I played for him. It was life-changing."

Shtern, Wilson says, wanted her to hold her violin differently, with the neck resting deep in the space between her left thumb and index finger. "I have to say the first two weeks were two of the worst weeks of my life," she says, "because when you grow up doing something — I was 28 — it was like starting over. I only saw black. And then it started to get better, and the end result is it's a lot more freedom, a lot more relaxing." In fact, Wilson wound up leaving Italy "to come study with Abram" in Los Angeles.

Violin pedagogy is passed down from teacher to student in part verbally and in part by demonstration. Violin masters have direct contact with younger generations, as they encounter them in master classes, and are sought out by up-and-coming players seeking guidance and their imprimatur. As Wilson puts it: "Shtern has continued to be involved with today's concertizing violinists, has developed relationships with the younger generation, such as Julian Rachlin and Vadim Repin. I know that when Repin is in town" — as he will be this week for a concert Saturday at Royce Hall — "he goes to Abram's house to visit with him and always gives him tickets to his performances."

BOW TECHNIQUE

Shtern's reputation was reflected in the high caliber of students presented to him during a public master class he taught in Montecito. A young Korean violinist, for instance, played the daunting third movement from the Sibelius Violin Concerto, after which Shtern and Emanuel Borok, the Dallas Symphony concertmaster and Shtern's translator, tried to communicate a different bowing to her. But clearly the student did not understand the request.

"Does she speak English?" Borok asked the festival's director, violinist Chan Ho Yun, who was seated across the room from the two Russians. Yun shook his head and quickly made his way to a seat next to Borok. Shtern then played the Sibelius section with the bowing he had recommended and Borok explained it in English to Yun, who translated Borok's explanation into Korean. The student smiled, now understanding what was being asked of her, and complied. Everyone in the audience breathed a sigh of relief.

Alexander Treger, the Los Angeles Philharmonic concertmaster and conductor of the Crossroads School Orchestra, was a student of David Oistrakh at the Moscow Conservatory in the late '60s and early '70s. "It was considered the top conservatory in the world," he recalls, with Oistrakh, fellow violinist Leonid Kogan and cellist Mstislav Rostropovich "all in the same building." Nevertheless, he often heard: "'Let's take a train to see Abrasha'" — the Russian nickname for "Abram." "'He knows how to do this, he knows how to do that.' Or, 'I'm going to Kiev. I'm going to see Abrasha. I need to find the right sound. He's going to help me.'"

Polesitsky, who went to Shtern in 1974, explains: "If you can imagine, for all of us in the Soviet Union, 'freedom' was not the most popular word, even in violin school. Everyone was teaching in a very standardized way. Abram kind of overturned all of that. The most important aspect for him is freedom. He was kind of a guru of freedom."

Says Kirillov: "If you stand on stage like a statue, as if you're going to lift a very heavy weight or something like that, you cannot play. Your approach when you come out on the stage to play a concert, it's not like you're going to beat some world record. This is what he told me. It's like you come out and you say, 'People, let me tell you something.'"

Given that the violin is an instrument famous for its hazards, a teacher who promises stress-free playing is either a charlatan or a miracle worker. But for Polesitsky, "Abram was showing by his phenomenal playing that such a freedom was within our reach. There were no shoulder rests, which he called crutches, no special mechanical movements, just a surprisingly easy, under-his-guidance search for a free, open sound and a natural, relaxed left hand."

Today, three months after the tribute in Montecito — where there were also two recitals in his honor, one given by students and the other by faculty members — Shtern is back home in West Hollywood. He may be nearly 90, but he's still au courant. He can even be seen on YouTube playing Fritz Kreisler's "Liebesleid" accompanied by his granddaughter Valeria Morgovskaya, one of the most sought-after accompanists in town. Morgovskaya lives within walking distance of her grandfather. Their neighborhood is full of storefronts with advertisements in Russian, and the chance of running into former Shevchenko opera stars at the local market is high.

SOVIET CONDUCTOR SURPASSES TRANSLATION

Working with a great conductor is not a common event. But, like the thrill of seeing the Kirov, it is an experience to treasure when it happens
May 27, 1986

THE local musicians selected to play during the Kirov Ballet's one-week engagement here had one day of rehearsal preceding the first *Swan Lake* last Wednesday. In the rehearsal room on the third floor of Shrine Auditorium the orchestra assembled early, eager to begin.

At the rehearsal, an intense, boyish-looking, diminutive man snuffed out his cigarette and took his place on the podium.

"This is the conductor," a large blond woman announced, with a rolled Russian "r" at the end of *conductor*. She sat down directly behind him for future translation responsibilities.

If any musician among us had yawned over the prospect of playing for yet another full-length production of *Swan Lake*, that sentiment was corrected a moment later at the downbeat.

Our "conductorrr" was Evgeny Kolobov, a 40-year-old man

who joined the Kirov five years ago. Like an actor preparing for his role, Kolobov's face clouded over with seriousness as he began the opening sweeping bars of the score.

As the intensity increased, our maestro's breathing became audible, an occasional hum perceptible. From the moment Kolobov submerged himself and us in Tchaikovsky's prelude, it was clear that he had superb stick technique. Nothing is ambivalent in it, or left to chance. He is easy to follow.

Technique without musicianship is not inspiring. A *rubato* —a stretching here of the line to sustain a phrase, a momentary acceleration there for tension—all were so heartfelt and genuine that the orchestra instantly responded to him. At the first break the musicians gathered into exuberant little groups of discussion. "That's how it should be!" a woodwind player said.

Later, the violins began a romantic passage. Kolobov stopped us, and to demonstrate what was missing he stroked his face with the palm of his hand in a loving caress. We played it again. With that gesture, the passage had been stripped of any aggressiveness and was now pure, gentle lyricism.

The orchestra was momentarily jarred from the proceedings when a group of men, some in gray suits, others in navy, appeared in the doorway, to observe us.

Our concertmaster began his cadenza. Kolobov heard it through, pressed both hands to his heart, his face scrunched up as if about to cry. He shook his hand warmly. "*Kak vas zavoot?*" (What is your name?), translated by one of our own Russian-speaking members of the orchestra.

"Ken."

This is the first time we'd heard Kolobov speak. In spite of seeing his translator behind him, we were startled by this sudden reminder of the language barrier. Until this point extended verbal communication had been unnecessary.

"Ken," he repeated tentatively and then burst into impassioned, fast Russian.

"You may take as much time as you want there. It is your moment," a Russian-speaking violinist translated. Ken Yerke nodded and began again. Kolobov's shoulders and thick square eyebrows raised with pleasure.

"*Prekrasna*" (wonderful), he murmured.

A little later we played a light dance which was not quite happy-go-lucky enough. He stopped us and pantomimed a carefree style. "Los Angeles!" he said, with an impish grin.

The rehearsal lasted from 10 a.m. to 5:30 p.m. Normally we would have been exhausted. We were exhilarated. We broke for dinner and went home to change into our concert black.

Everyone was instructed to wear a Kirov identity badge at all times. Failure to display it would mean non-admittance to the building. To get back to the pit, orchestra members had to walk through a mine field of about 20 men, some dressed in navy and some in gray. Clustered in small groups according to suit color, engrossed in intense conversation, eyeing everyone who passed by, they didn't appear to be typical balletomanes.

The unconfirmed rumor was that the ones in gray were Soviets, those in navy, State Department. Except for dancers coming and going directly onstage, the backstage area was conspicuously lacking in ballet ambiance.

We returned to work. Kolobov had prepared us well. True to his style, no motion was unnecessary or unjustified. His eyes expressed the pathos, terror, gaiety, gravity—whatever mood was required as he coaxed out of the orchestra the effects needed.

His gestures were unhampered by histrionics. Like a magnificent marionetteer, Kolobov's control of the various elements was never in doubt and yet his presence remained unobtrusive. Lest it be forgotten that the orchestra was secondary to what went on on stage, the dancers were met with wild applause.

At the end of the entire performance Kolobov placed his hands on his heart and smiled at us. His sincerity was absolute.

VIVALDI IN A TIME OF WAR

Beverly Hills teacher finds violin and Vivaldi in a time of war
November 2, 2014

I teach violin in Beverly Hills, and this summer I received an unusual request.

Jonathan Hollander, a choreographer and founder of the nearly 40-year-old Battery Dance Company in New York, contacted me through mutual friends. Hollander was looking for a violin teacher for a 24-year-old student in Erbil, Iraq.

What persuaded me to accept was that "this particular student's heart was broken when he couldn't continue to take violin lessons."

Hollander is not naive. He subscribes to Leonard Bernstein's philosophy: "Art never stopped a war... art cannot change events. But it can change people." Battery Dance Company's educational program Dancing to Connect has been conducted in more than 40 conflict zones, including Iraqi Kurdistan, where the company's teaching artists have brought together Kurds, Shia, Sunni and Christians. They've had workshops with mixed groups of Israelis and Palestinians. As Hollander says: "You can't dance with some-one you distrust."

Others also have used cultural diplomacy to help sort out conflict. In 1999, Daniel Barenboim and the late Edward Said founded their West-Eastern Divan Orchestra, bringing together young Israelis and Palestinians and other Arabs.

Hollander's latest enterprise is to match private teachers with students in war-torn countries. Since I began teaching my student, whom I will call Mustafa for his protection, Hollander has taken on mentoring a young choreographer in Baghdad and arranged for Diane Walsh, a concert pianist in Portland, Maine, to begin teaching an advanced piano student in Erbil.

Curious about a student desperate to continue violin lessons in the midst of chaos, I checked out Mustafa's Facebook page. It shows a handsome, laid-back-looking young man with his beloved violin beside him. He could be anywhere in the world.

In an email, Mustafa acknowledged that he had not touched his violin in months, "too busy about ISIS. Bad people don't want to listen to music. No energy to play. We have a bad situation in my country as every one in the world knows about the war in Iraq but it isn't my reason because I don't count myself an Iraqi person, I am Kurdish and I live in Kurdistan which is a free region in Iraq. I like you teach me on Skype and I have computer in my room."

Erbil had never been on my radar, but I suddenly found myself reading everything I could about the capital of Kurdistan; like the rest of the world, I was also glued to the news there. Steve Coll in the New Yorker writes that since the American invasion of Iraq, this region "has been the most stable place in an unstable country."

We scheduled the first lesson for Aug. 12, but almost immediately, the Islamic State, ISIS, ISIL, IS — the jihadist group whose name seemed to change daily — took center stage, hacking its way across the region. As the world stared, the radical group went after the biggest dam in Iraq, near Mosul, 50 miles from Erbil.

Hollander emailed me: "The situation might be exploding and communication could be too dangerous for your student and his family." After the initial flurry of emails from Mustafa, there was suddenly nothing. Given the events unfolding in Kurdistan, I assumed violin lessons were not going to happen. I managed to reach Mustafa on his cellphone; he told me the Internet was temporarily down.

Yet I detected no doubt on his part that lessons would go ahead. "See you on Aug. 20 at 9 a.m.," I said.

"Inshallah," Mustafa replied.

All hell was breaking loose around Erbil, but on Aug. 20 at 9:02 a.m. California time, Mustafa was there, apologizing for being late.

His brown and black violin, made by a local luthier, sounded better than it looked. In the middle of his three-octave G Major scale, the lights went off and I was left looking and listening to a very earnest, bearded young man illuminated by the light of his computer.

The room he was in was stark white, with no visible furniture, though his computer must have been on a chair or table. I'm not sure how long he has been playing — maybe four years, since he's a graduate of the Institute of Fine Arts, a college in Baghdad.

A minute or so later, the lights came back on. The Skype connection broke several times, but we persevered. I heard some arpeggios and talked to him about bow speed, legato, tone, shifting and intonation. I encouraged him to play the scale as if it were the most beautiful music in the world. "Be brave," I told him. "Use the entire bow."

It was impossible to put out of my mind that not far from this room where my student worked to improve his tone and acquire more technique, thousands of Yazidis had taken refuge on a desert mountaintop as they tried to escape Islamic State. On Aug. 18, two days before our first lesson, the Americans had come back into Iraq, after a two-year absence, to launch airstrikes in an effort to help the Kurds and Iraqis take back the dam near Mosul, as well as to protect American oil interests.

"Can you straighten your wrist?" I asked, maneuvering my left wrist from a bent position, palm to the ceiling, into a straight line.

"No," he told me firmly. There was clearly no room for negotiation.

"It will give your fingers the freedom to get around the violin," I told him, not unaware of the political overtones in my choice of words.

I played the opening octaves and broken thirds of Beethoven's violin concerto to show him how fast the fingers could move if positioned correctly, hovering over the strings. His eyes widened.

"No," he told me again. "Change too hard." I let it go for now.

Then out of the blue, he blurted out: "I hate classical music." I had trouble believing that. I played for him the first and second movements of *Winter* from the Vivaldi *Seasons*, which he hadn't heard before, playing into the computer, to a captive audience of one. I promised to send him a YouTube of the complete Vivaldi concertos.

"Could you teach me about pop music?" Mustafa asked.

I know nothing about current pop music and wondered what exactly he meant by "pop." I suddenly broke into Petula Clark's "Downtown."

"I crazy about this!" he shouted.

At the end of the lesson, he said: "It's amazing time, really. You give me your time. Thank you so much."

"See you next week."

"Inshallah."

A week later, I wondered whether Mustafa would turn up for his lesson. In a way, he was like any other transfer student, in that I had to figure out what he needed most and in what order. On the other hand, he was in a crazy situation, on the outskirts of a very undefined, unconventional war zone.

It was Aug. 27, 9 a.m. in California, and there he was, right on the dot. We picked up where we had left off.

"Are you sure it's OK to take violin lessons with an American?" I asked.

"I have good place for security," he assured me.

"Can you help me technique to speed my finger?" he asked.

"Make an umbrella with your fingers," I told him, as I turned my upper body so he could see my straight forearm and left hand fingers over the fingerboard. He shot me a look.

"If you want to be able to move your fingers quickly..." I said, moving my fingers rapidly to prove my point.

He straightened his wrist, repeated the exercise and looked at his fingers in amazement.

I wanted him to have an etude book, and I held the book close to the computer screen so he could see the title. He disappeared, then reappeared, grinning, and gave me the thumbs-up sign as he held an ancient copy of the same music, Wohlfahrt written in big letters, with Kurdish letters above.

My next student was about to arrive.

"Listen, about pop music..."

"It's OK. I like classical music...," he brushed me off. He had listened to the Vivaldi "Seasons." "I crazy about this Vivaldi — good producer."

"Composer?"

"Composer," he said, making a mental note of it.

On the spur of the moment, I played "Over the Rainbow." He

practically started dancing, he was so happy.

"I crazy about this" he said, beaming.

So I could teach him about pop music — from the last century.

My next student, an 11-year-old boy, and his mother walked in. I introduced them on Skype. Mustafa was thrilled to meet a student of mine in Los Angeles. "That's just amazing," my student's mother said as she wiped a tear from under her sunglasses. I explained to her son that this violin student was in northern Iraq. He shrugged.

It was hard to get Mustafa out of my mind. As a violin teacher, I am used to students graduating or moving on for one reason or another. Some stay in touch, some are never heard from again. No one's life was ever in danger, as far as I knew. Anything could happen to Mustafa, and who would tell the violin teacher 7,000 miles away?

As a violin teacher, I'd never thought at the end of a lesson that I might not see a student again.

At his third lesson, on Sept. 3, Mustafa told me that he was prepared to join the Peshmerga (armed Kurdish fighters). While military service in Kurdistan is voluntary and he'd never served, he said: "I can go to fighting. They not conquer my country."

Mustafa asked me if I'd heard about the journalist (James Foley) from the United States who had recently been beheaded. I nodded.

"I cried about this," he told me. He looked as if he were going to break down again.

"Let me hear your etude," I said, changing the subject.

A week or so later, Hollander emailed me. "Have you seen Mustafa's latest Facebook photos?"

There he was in military fatigues and boots, surrounded by other recruits, draped in the flag of Kurdistan, the violin nowhere to be seen. He canceled his fourth lesson. "Very busy," he emailed.

HOW I LEARNED TO LOVE OPERA

When New York teachers went on strike in 1968 I became a reluctant student of Puccini's La Bohème
Jan 16, 2019

I was a 16-year-old student at the High School of Music and Art in New York when the city's teachers began a series of walk-outs in 1968 that continued for months. There was no way I was going to cross a picket line, so like thousands of other kids I was left with a lot of time on my hands.

Those days have been on my mind this week, as I've thought about Los Angeles students during the current teachers' strike.

I was a serious violin student, so one option for me, as my teachers were manning the picket line, was to spend more time practicing.

My older brother had a better idea. He had graduated from the University of Iowa a few months earlier and was home trying to write and figure out his next move. He proposed teaching two courses, with me as his sole pupil: one on Shakespeare, the other on Puccini.

"I'll take the Shakespeare one," I told him, "but I'll pass on Puccini. I'm not into opera."

"Let me play you one thing," he said.

He gently removed a record from its sleeve and placed *La Bohème* on the turntable. Then he carefully moved the needle to "Musetta's Waltz."

When the track was over, my mind was changed. "OK, I'll try it."

My brother has always had this effect on me. Once, when I was 14 and we were boarding the No. 4 bus to go to the Cloisters, he asked me: "What do you know about Nicholas II?"

"Nothing, and I'm not interested," I replied, knowing he would happily fill our hour-long trip with a lecture.

"All right then, I won't tell you about Rasputin, or Alexei or…"

"OK, OK, tell me about all of it," I relented.

Years later, I got a degree in Slavic languages at UCLA.

I don't know what my fellow students did during the New York teachers' strike, but each morning, my brother held a seminar to discuss *Romeo and Juliet*, *Macbeth*, *Hamlet* and *A Midsummer Night's Dream*, complete with exams. He relished that part.

Recently I came across some of those exams. After one of my answers, he had scribbled, "Clearly you haven't read the question carefully."

In the afternoons, we listened to and discussed *La Bohème*. I couldn't get enough of it. I had been raised on a wide variety of classical music, including vocal music. But opera had always seemed inexplicable and off-putting, with silly plots and outsized characters. I had made no attempt to climb inside it.

My brother changed that.

One night, at dinner, he announced that, since I had taken my final exam in *La Bohème*, we would be beginning *Tosca* the next day.

"No, I'm not ready!" I protested.

Our parents had been extremely tolerant as *La Bohème* blared from the living room day after day, but now they embraced my brother's new lesson plan. "We're ready!" they said in unison.

So the next day we began my second opera, which I adored just as much as the first.

In the end, the New York teachers' strike of 1968 hooked me for life on opera. Even as I pursued my degree at UCLA, I earned money as a freelance violinist, often playing opera. I have also taught opera classes myself, introducing others to Puccini's "Musetta's Waltz," which still makes me feel as if my heart is going to explode, and moving on to a range of other operas, including my brother's favorite, *Carmen*.

I still play my CD of the stupendous performance of "Musetta's Waltz" that my brother first played for me, with Victoria de Los Angeles and Jussi Bjorling.

I certainly hope the Los Angeles teachers' strike will be brief. I hope the teachers get what they need so they can provide the best education for their students.

But I also hope there are some remarkable older siblings out there with time on their hands.

CHICAGO
FRANCIS FORD COPPOLA PRESENTS
ABEL GANCE'S NAPOLEON
FRANCIS COPPOLA
PRESENTS
ABEL GANCE'S
"NAPOLEON"
ORCHESTRA
OF ILLINOIS
CONDUCTED BY
CARMINE COPPOLA

PLAYING IN THE *NAPOLEON* ORCHESTRA: THE VIEW FROM THE VIOLIN SECTION

The author played in the first violin section of the orchestra for the recent Napoleon *showing at the Shrine Auditorium.*
August 23, 1981

THE consensus among the 60 members of the pit is that playing *Napoleon* was one of the most physically draining jobs ever. It's not that the Carmine Coppola score of Abel Gance's 1927 silent film is difficult but that it's constant. Four hours. Or the equivalent of playing two full symphony concerts back-to-back.

Bursitis, tendinitis and general aches and pains are frequent complaints among musicians and they abounded in this pit. Lips hurt in the brass and woodwind sections and arms were ready to drop in the strings. Simply holding up the violin, one of the most awkward instruments to play, for a long period of time is exhausting.

With *Napoleon* the audience seemed immeasurably appreciative of the orchestra's physical workout.

On my way to the stage door one night, some eager patrons asked whether I had rested up for the performance–they had heard that it was very demanding.

One man, obviously familiar with, shall I say, "the pitfalls" of string playing, addressed a group of us after the show: "My God! How's the old bow arm? Think you'll recover by Christmas?" he asked.

The newspaper ads for *Napoleon* noted that the film was accompanied by a live 60-piece orchestra-and, indeed, when we went into the pit we were for the most part alive and kicking.

The pit itself was tightly crammed with musicians and their instruments and accessories. Warm to begin with, the temperature in the Shrine Auditorium rose higher still with the rigorous physical exertion required to bring off the music. Joking among members of the pit included the idea that this would be the ideal time to begin a diet, and that we should be weighed in before and after each performance.

Contrary to the general feeling that we wouldn't survive to the very end of each performance, we in fact did.

Somewhere around the three-hour mark one felt unable to continue. But like a marathon runner, there was a second burst of energy. I even experienced the equivalent of the runner's "high" in which I felt I could play forever. Anyone want to hear it again? Right now? No problem!

What made the viewing of *Napoleon* unique was the combination of the live musical ensemble coupled with the "dead" medium of film. Particularly wonderful was the audience's response to the "event." Their enthusiasm was an inspiration.

There was also a fascinating switch that took place. The orchestra was keenly aware of the audience's response. We heard them and in some cases we saw them. In a sense the orchestra became the audience to the audience's own performance.

Audiences differed nightly. Some moments were roared at one night and quietly chuckled at the next. Some jumped to their feet for a standing ovation after Act I, others were more restrained. Our second performance was generally felt by members of the pit to have dragged a bit. Everything seemed slower. It could not possibly have been. More likely we were responding to the night after opening night, traditionally a letdown. The third night picked up again.

Looking up from the pit to the first row a few feet above us, one saw the whites of people's eyes. Everyone was riveted to the screen–almost mesmerized. There was only one night I was aware that some of us were disturbed by talking. Next to part of the violin section were two couples who discussed every detail between them as though they were in their own living room, watching TV. They seemed thoroughly oblivious to the orchestra's "liveness" and to the fact that we were performing.

The height of the comedy was reached when one of the women loudly said something to her friend across her temporarily silent husband. The friend couldn't make out what she had said. We had heard her loud and clear. Finally the friend shouted above a very loud section in the Berlioz excerpt, "What?" I had a hard time playing I was laughing so hard.

Another night about an hour after the film began, a man in the audience stood up and apparently walked out. I don't know whether anyone else in the orchestra noticed. I felt dreadful. It seemed as if he had hardly given the film a chance. I was delighted a few minutes later when the same man briskly made his way back to his seat.

The most bewildering aspect of the experience was hearing about moments in the film from friends. People assumed we knew what was going on when essentially we hadn't the foggiest idea. I asked some friends to let me know who the man in the powdered Mozartean wig was because I dreamed about him one night. He turned out to be Robespierre.

What little I knew of what was happening on the screen was derived from seeing parts of it during our brief rest sections, from hearing about it from friends, or from knowing a section of music from memory enough to peek at the screen. About half of the orchestra was situated under the lip of the stage where it was impossible to view the screen, but my seat was at the outer edge of the pit.

In an organ solo during which the rest of the orchestra relaxes, those who could watched the screen. My eyes met those of a violinist at the back of the pit.

"You mean you can't see a thing?" I mouthed to him across the second violin section.

"No." He shook his head with resignation. "I watch you watching," he replied good-naturedly.

Someday I hope to see *Napoleon* in its present state. Until then, I am in a curious position. I eagerly asked friends at the end, "Did you like it"? But, in fact, I don't know what "it" really is, having never fully experienced it.

For our second series of performances we lost a few regulars and gained some newcomers. These players seemed stunned by the audience's response something the rest of us had grown accustomed to. They had been warned about the endless sixteenth notes, the spent bow arms, sore backs, but no one had detailed our pleasure derived from the audience's euphoria–the standing ovations, bravo and encore shouting.

Every night when we wended our way out of the cavernous basement into the cool night air we were greeted by friendly audience members who thanked us for working so hard. They seemed very aware of the physical stamina required. One man said to me after one Sunday matinee:

"I can't believe you are playing another performance this evening!"

"God! What a thought!" I answered. "We're not!"

NOW YOU'RE HOT, NOW YOU'RE NOT

WHEN a film and its soundtrack are artistically in sync, it's impossible to contemplate one without the other. Leonard Bernstein's score for *On the Waterfront* adds a dimension that elevates the film to nearly operatic proportions. Luke Skywalker's adventures in space are given a turbulent grandeur by John Williams' full orchestral score. In both cases, the marriage of sound and image proved not only felicitous, but memorable.

Inappropriate music, on the other hand, can throw a whole scene off, even snuff out the ambience of an entire film. Imagine the shower scene in *Psycho*, not with composer Bernard Herrmann's piercing, staccato violins–but with tubas. Normally, of course, strings mean romance. Anyone who's sat in a movie theater knows the formula: brass for nobility, timpani for danger, etc. But here, the aural oxymoron was just right.

It takes a particularly crafty and attuned composer to find those right aural atmospheres. And since much of a film's longevity has to do with the quality of its score, proven film composers – or at least those who are on a roll at the box office–often enjoy the cushiest gigs in all composer-dom. A hot composer is one who's at the top of a studio's roster, chooses what projects he wants rather than taking whatever is offered, and is associated with name directors and astronomical grosses. A few of the anointed, like John Williams (*Jaws, Star Wars, E. T.*), may even win an audience of their own, have their own loyal fans. The great composers of history have routinely cleaved to patrons, and if Hollywood execs aren't exactly Medicis, they can often lure some of today's finest musical talent.

The Academy Award-winning scorers who started out in the '30s–Alfred Newman (*The Song of Bernadette*), Miklos Rozsa (*Ben Hur*), Erich Wolfgang Korngold (*The Adventures of Robin Hood*) and Franz Waxman (*Sunset Boulevard*) were inspired by the great symphonic composers of the late 19th and early 20th centuries. But more versatility is demanded of today's film composers, who must take the very latest in pop music, fuse it with state-of-the-art synthesizer technology and mix in an idiomatic knowledge of traditional orchestral scores. You name it, they've got to write for it. As with most '80s art forms, eclecticism is the name of the game. There's never been a time in film history when so many different types of music were being written concurrently, and by such an enormously varied group of composers.

Of the roughly 200 film composers working in Hollywood today, there is considerable consensus among studio cognoscenti and filmmakers as to who are the hottest. While not necessarily the best, they are the ones most in demand just now. But being hot this summer doesn't guarantee anyone from freezing in a fickle industry by next winter. Although these "arriving" composers come from various musical past lives, what they have in common is being white, male–and young. Today's hotshot steps up to the sound-stage podium, baton in hand, having landed his first low-budget feature while still baby-faced enough to aggravate a recording studio full of well-seasoned musicians, many of whom played for Rozsa, Newman, Korngold and company. There are myriad paths from mailroom obscurity to becoming one of the Chosen. Perhaps the most direct route is to be associated with an unmitigated smash. When *Beverly Hills Cop* turned out to be a blockbuster, it cata-pulted a relatively unknown composer named Harold Faltermeyer onto the Most Wanted list. Faltermeyer's subsequent successes with *Top Gun* and *Beverly Hills Cop II* further demonstrated his ability to write ultra-hip, instantly likable, catchy melodic lines–propelling him to his own top position in the business.

Some composers are more in demand before a film comes out than after. It was considered a major coup getting Thomas Dolby, an English rock phenom whose "She Blinded Me With Science" was a huge MTV hit, to participate in scoring *Howard the Duck* – restlessly anticipated as a block buster. That was before *Howard* came out sans splash and promptly drowned. (There was, by the way, a last ditch effort to save the film by the laying of several other hands onto the score.) The trick is to be signed for your next movie before your current eggs hatch. Dolby had already signed on for Ken Russell's *Gothic* when *Howard* flopped.

Though no substitute for talent or perseverance, connections can come in handy – and none better than blood lines. Second gener-ation film composers Thomas Newman (*Desperately Seeking Susan*) and his brother David (*Critters*) carry on the family enterprise of father Alfred (*How The West Was Won*) and Uncle Lionel (*Cheaper By the Dozen*). They are joined by cousin Randy (*The Natural*). Other dynasties in the making are Jerry Goldsmith (*Patton*) and son Joel (*The Man With Two Brains*), and Elmer Bernstein (*To Kill A Mockingbird*) and his son Peter (*My Science Project*).

Tom and David Newman didn't have the benefit of their father's mentorship – he died when they were teenagers. Tom is one of the few composers who writes in a style loosely labeled (not by Tom) "New Age". Rather than commenting overtly on the drama of specific scenes, Tom brings to his writing a hip edge that creates an overall color and texture for each picture. On the other hand, David, who was first a violinist and conductor, is more clearly carrying on the Alfred Newman tradition of underlining the dramatic action and using a full-size orchestra (versus Tom's synthesizers). Considered more akin to James Horner and John Williams, David Newman's music has the mature, lavish sound of someone who has been writing grand orchestral scores for years.

When Peter Bernstein decided to pursue film scoring, he worked for his father as an orchestrator (deciding what instruments should play what in a score). Elmer eventually lost his orchestrator as Peter took on projects of his own. While still maintaining a sensibility shared with his father (the importance of a memorable melody), Peter ventures into additional arenas, blending synthesizers and pop textures into traditional orchestral soundtracks.

Ultimately, dynastic credentials are no insurance. For Peter Bernstein, "Being someone's son is irrelevant. It's the leap of faith that's the brave thing. Someone's got to have the guts to give you a break. The quest for young people helps."

Then there's the rock route: parlaying one's glory from live performance and records into celluloid. The greatest breeding ground for the majority of film composers is the pop world. Former or current rock stars are a highly esteemed commodity. The hope of the studio executives who hire them is that they will segue from pop stardom to film score superstardom. Such was the case of Randy Newman, Danny Elfman of Oingo Boingo and Stewart Copeland of the Police. Tomorrow's hot scorers may include the Police's Andy Summers (*Down and Out in Beverly Hills*), Carly Simon (*Heartburn*), AC/DC (*Maximum Overdrive*) and Toto (*Dune*).

Randy Newman's film music, which bears little resemblance to his best-known songs, is traditionally orchestral, with no less the subtle wit and strong melodic sense. Ironically, Danny Elfman's (*Pee-Wee's Big Adventure, Back to School, Wisdom*) rock baptism has had less impact on his frenetic, jauntily humorous scores than has his emulation of Bernard Herrmann (*Citizen Kane, Psycho, Taxi Driver*) and Fellini's music man, Nino Rota. Stewart Copeland creates scores that emphasize creative rhythmic tracks boasting unusual and clever use of percussion. Although associated with only two films – Francis Coppola's *Rumble Fish* and Richard Tuggle's *Out of Bounds* – Copeland is still considered bankable by virtue of his rank in the pop world.

Not everyone agrees that bringing musicians from another medium into film scoring is such a good idea. When the late Bernard Herrmann was asked what he thought of the intrusion of rock artists into film composing, he answered "They're not getting instant composers. They're just getting a lot more garbage. And it is not worth including in a serious discussion about film music. After all, if we're going to discuss a novel, we don't talk about comic books, do we?"

Despite Herrmann's sentiment, shared by many older composers who lament the decline of formal training for their skills, there are those who have managed to survive the ravages of fashion and remain in constant demand: Henry Mancini (*The Pink Panther, That's Life*), John Barry (*Goldfinger, Out of Africa*), Maurice Jarre (*Doctor Zhivago, The Mosquito Coast*) and Dave Grusin (*Candy,*

Ishtar). And then there is the protean, undauntable Elmer Bernstein, who in the '50s composed jazz scores like *The Man with the Golden Arm*, and in the '60s did orchestral soundtracks like *The Magnificent Seven*. Bernstein has had the capacity to adapt once again, having lately become unofficial resident scorer for the comedies of both John Landis (*Animal House, Three Amigos*) and Ivan Reitman (*Ghostbusters, Legal Eagles*). Tracking the careers of film music veterans is one way of perceiving changes in the way the game is played. Asking someone on the business end is another. According to Richard Kraft, vice president of Varese-Saraband Records, a label specializing in current and classic film scores, "In the '30s a composer was hired by the music head of the studio. He himself was a musician. Assignment to a picture was based purely on the dramatic needs of the movie. Composers were under contract to the studio. The head of the music knew each composer's work and who would be right for which films. Now the role of studio music head is in the hands of the filmmakers and music V.P.'s. Currently no music department head has a traditional music background – They've all been pulled from the record industry. The music V.P.'s main requirement is to serve the movie and simultaneously produce a successful soundtrack album."

The success of film scores observes what at first appear to be arbitrary laws. A particular music fitted to a particular image either works or it doesn't. After the fact we can look back and see that some novelty – one of the many styles buzzing around – "took" and dominated an era. In the early days of cinema a lone piano lent a hand to the events on screen. Then scores issued from the huge orchestras of the '30s and '40s, the jazz of the '50s, the pop music of the '60s. With the 1981 Academy Award-winning soundtrack for *Chariots of Fire*, Greek composer Vangelis introduced an all-synthesizer score that was to resound in everything that followed.

The arrival of the synthesizer has been celebrated by some producers, studio executives and even composers for its alleged cost-effectiveness – based on the highly debatable contention that the budget of a film is drastically reduced by hiring one man and his machines rather than expending a plural number of musicians' fees. Though the equation is not so simple, it can't be denied that what the synthesizer has done is to bring up-to-date electronic pop into the here-and-now of film scoring. And it is largely as a result of the electronic influx that film music can no longer be accused of its customary lag behind pop culture, and behind the very modern techniques of filmmaking itself. Let's face it, 19th century-style music is often more appropriate in films for discerning adults than it is in the summer escape flicks of 13-year-old TV addicts.

It has been rumored that the synthesizer threatens to replace the live orchestra altogether. Proponents of the Synclavier and the Fairlight – synthesizers that can reproduce acoustic and electronic instruments by means of digital sampling – feel certain that this technology will even do away with the 400-year-old wooden box called the Stradivarius. Still, most composers, while making liberal use of electronic equipment, acknowledge the inability of a machine to do a human's work – that is, to duplicate the nuances of an acoustic instrument and its living, breathing, highly trained player. So as not to lose this ineffable aural poetry, most film scorers use a combination of man-made and programmed sound, resulting in an extended – rather than dehumanized–palette of musical hues and textures.

Nevertheless, there are composers who specialize in electronic fare, like the German-born Sylvester Levay, a synthesist whose credits include *Cobra*, Whoopie Goldberg's *Burglar*, and the music direction of *Saturday Night Live*. Levay comes out of the Georgio Moroder stable of film composers (as did Harold Faltermeyer).

Moroder, whose scoring company, the Music Team, produces film soundtracks, grooms his composers in much the same way Roger Corman has nurtured young directors in his singular, unorthodox school of film making. Unlike standard, staid film-school training, the Corman and Moroder system gives hands-on experience.

Though he writes acoustic music as well, Brad Fiedel is considered one of the top synthesizer composers. Having done five features in the last year and a half, he's certainly plugged in. Fiedel, who comes from generations of musicians, is a self-described "film buff who likes to get into the backbone of the picture." Nothing is out of bounds in his instrumentation. Whether it calls for a string quartet or banging a frying pan with a hammer, Fiedel's game. Noted for his innovative concoctions of effects and intelligent mixing of electronic, acoustic and vocal tracks, Fiedel has been cautious not to repeat himself by carefully selecting different types of films to score. *Fright Night, Compromising Positions* and *Desert Bloom* are three on his wide-ranging list of credits.

Although not exclusively a synthesist, the composer most heavily associated with the use of the Synclavier for film scoring is Alan Silvestri. Silvestri has brought his enormous versatility to a purely synthetic approach in creating the moods and atmosphere for such diverse projects as *Romancing the Stone, Back to the Future, Clan of the Cave Bear* and *No Mercy.*

Like other artists who exploit themselves in order to cash in on their momentary place in the sun, some successful young film composers realize that their time may be limited. With the success of *Risky Business* in 1983, the German electronic group Tangerine Dream was extremely hot in film. They were one of the first all-synthesizer groups, and their 30 previous albums ensured an enormous built-in crossover audience for any new soundtrack. It was Tangerine Dream who wrote a second score replacing Jerry

Goldsmith original for Ridley Scott's *Legend* ("the last act of a desperate man," noted an inside source). Goldsmith (*Platoon, Chinatown)* is considered one of the best in the business, hailed on both sides of any net. If a studio realizes that it's about to release a bomb, the last resort (short of rewriting and reshooting, which is rarely done) is often to fire the composer and replace the score. Bernard Herrmann, responding to an emergency telegram from Darryl Zanuck to rescue a film in distress, cabled "I can dress the corpse, but I can't bring it back to life." (*Legend,* by the way, beat a hasty retreat from the movie theatres despite Tangerine Dream's efforts. Considered by many to be passé their film score popularity seems to be undergoing a cooling trend. They're presently scoring *Shy People,* the new Jill Clayburgh film. At one time they scored between five and ten films a year.)

It's too early to say who among these composers "have legs." Alfred Newman, Miklos Rozsa and Bernard Herrmann had legs, had staying power. Staying on top is a balancing act – maintaining a reputation for originality while at the same time not doing something so outlandish that you're considered quirky or unreliable. The competition's fierce, the pressure tremendous and the need to stay trendy relentless. But for these guys, it's all in a day's work.

Thirty-five-year-old Mark Isham did not set out to become a film composer but fell into it accidentally. Isham comes to film scoring via Windham Hill fame, a record label phenomenon in its own right. Enclosed in record jackets designed to impress coffee-table browsers as much as audiophiles, the original "sound" of Windham Hill was strictly shades of New Age mellow ("songs without words for the purpose of physical and spiritual healing). It is not to be confused with the Minimalist school, an intellectual cadre of the New Music movement that includes people like Philip Glass, Terry Riley and John Adams. New Age music is neither rock nor jazz. It's simple, naive, tranquilizing–with a distinct, but diluted, folk influence. It's the '80s answer to Andre Kostelanetz.

Isham, Windham Hill's first non-acoustic solo artist doesn't consider his music New Age. "New Age music doesn't challenge in a musical way whatsoever," he says. "I can't stand it. But I've been in this business too long to get uppity and arrogant about other people's approaches. New Age is not about writing the next concerto, making a pop single or giving people something to dance to. I'm more traditional. I love Mozart. I care about form, structure, complexity all those worries that aesthetics are built on."

While many of Isham's peers specialize in repetitive forms–at times gnawingly aimless–Isham's music, though highly rhythmic and atmospheric, is at the same time focused and melodic. Not that he doesn't acknowledge the value of repetition. "You have to look at the development of the synthesizer as a musical instrument to see where the compositional techniques come from. Short, repetitive patterns were some of the first things that early machines could do. So that's become part of the standard vocabulary for synthesizer music."

But Isham has gone beyond that. For one thing, the interchange of acoustic and synthetic instruments in his work is such that it is hard to discern where one begins and the other leaves off. The music is so skillfully woven that when it emerges out of unalloyed sound effects it often sounds as indigenous to the scene as the effects–themselves–and yet it remains haunting, subliminal music. "Electronics, if used at all, should add mystery. They should just change the sound in a way that you think, 'Boy, that's strange'–but you're not even aware of it. It's a visceral reaction."

How does Isham go about the job of scoring? "Initially, I like to not even worry about 'spotting cues' for a long time and just think about scoring for the movie as a whole. You think about the writing that would put the audience more where the movie is taking place than the movie itself is already doing. *Trouble in Mind* is a good example, because it's such an atmospheric film. You're in a world which is very different, and I think one of the successful things about the score is that it reinforces that.

"Then, as basic themes and ideas come out, I start to define the orchestra. In this day and age you can put anything together. It can be so huge—you don't want to just leave it open or you're going to get this completely disjointed, non-personality sort of sound. You want to define the sounds in the environment and then find sounds that reinforce that environment as it exists visually."

Isham's combination of musical talent and a strong visual sense is not surprising given his background. His mother is a professional violinist and his father a professor of art and music. Having already studied violin and piano until his early teens, Isham fell in love with the trumpet. A chance hearing of jazz on the radio and the subsequent influence of Miles Davis were to change his musical thinking forever. In the mid-'70s he joined the San Francisco Symphony. Working in jazz clubs until the wee hours of the morning followed by 10 a.m. symphony rehearsals finally forced him to relinquish the monkey suit for life on the road with both a rock band called the Sons of Champlain and jazz pianist Art Lande's group Rubisa Patrol. Somewhere in his travels he came across Morton Subotnick's avant-garde electronic music, which tipped him off to the last component of his musical education.

In 1982 director Carroll Ballard happened to hear a tape of Isham's music at the home of the poster artist doing the ads for his film *Never Cry Wolf*. Having already thrown out two scores for the film, Ballard was anxious to finish the film and hired Isham, who was then living in London. Thus began a cascade of credits that includes the Academy Award winning documentary *The Times of*

Harvey Milk, The Hitcher, Trouble in Mind, and Alan Rudolph's upcoming *Made in Heaven.*

One of the great advantages to Isham's soundtracks is that he is unhampered by what has come before him–he's an innocent blessed with a unique sensibility. There is a seamless overall texture to his scores, with no drastic telegraphing of scene changes, no "composer's message" blaring from the speakers. Rather, Isham's music breathes naturally with the narrative contours of the film.

Isham is unusual for the discretion with which he approaches film composing–his scores may for the most part have as much music as the next guy, but it seems as if there's less. In *Mrs. Soffel,* a period piece, Isham uses music sparingly, enhancing the tension, sadness, gloom and hope of the lovers. The orchestration is acoustic and electronic, with a plaintive piano overlay a subtly toned accompaniment that italicizes the film's melancholic ambience.

Besides pursuing a career in film, Isham continues to concertize as a solo trumpet player and synthesist. After years of touring with various groups, including Van Morrison and the Beach Boys, he now tours with eclectic ensembles of his own devising, where he ' 'gets to blow a little bit," according to one tour member.

Unlike Isham, whose scoring career is merely one aspect of his professional life, James Horner, 33, is a full-time film composer. Many filmmakers looking for a traditional orchestral score will hire him–not surprisingly, considering the film industry's youth fetish. The logic in hiring the ubiquitous Horner is that he may be more likely to turn in something fresh, given his zigzag, try-anything career: In a single year, he wrote an orchestral score for *Aliens,* a synthesizer score for *Where the River Runs Black,* an orchestral sounding electronic score for *The Name of the Rose,* an old-fashioned, sentimental score for the Spielberg animated feature *An American Tail,* and a steel-drum ethnic score for *Offbeat.* Not only a polymorphous composer, Horner is clearly a prolific one as well.

A graduate in piano and composition of the Royal College of Music in London, Horner received his master's degree in composition from USC. Pursuing the esoteric career of a composer, he suffered through concerts where his music was lumped into the category of New Music. In 1979, when Horner was teaching composition at UCLA while working toward his Ph.D. there, an AFI student heard one of his pieces at a concert and asked Horner to compose a score for his film. He was reluctant to comply, but, realizing how miserable he had been languishing in academic obscurity, he decided to give it a shot, and discovered a new calling. Seven years later, Horner has 34 feature films to his credit, including some of Hollywood 's highest-grossing films (*Star Trek II, 48 HRS., Cocoon*). Horner has a reputation for being soft-spoken but certainly not shy about expressing himself or his needs. "People say I'm arrogant. Why? Because I'm 33 years old and I have complete confidence in my music. I never worry about whether I'm happy with a cue. I only worry about selling it to a director because I know it's terrific. It all depends on the filmmaker—how conservative or liberal he is, how much he'll let me do. I always like to experiment a great deal, take a lot of chances, but it means running the risk of disaster. I insist on particular players, music mixers, studios—it's music casting. If you were making a pop record, no one would question your insistence on studio, mixer, artist. These are key elements. But here they say, 'Horner's arrogant.'"

WAGNER
COPLAND
STRAUSS
BIZET
PROKOFIEV

TEMP TRACK

Battling for the Score
August 12, 1986

GIVEN the youthful profile of today's market, the importance of a film's score has gone far beyond setting tone and pacing. For the independent producer on a tight budget, the right soundtrack can mean millions of dollars in free advertising and publicity (in addition to retail sales). Getting it right may hinge on the director's choice of temp tracks.

Imagine the shower scene in *Psycho* without the piercing violin screeches of Bernard Herrmann's score. Or Zeffirelli's *Romeo and Juliet* lacking its romantic love theme. Or Luke Skywalker's destruction of the Death Star missing John Williams' sweeping orchestral sound.

When a movie "works," you are too absorbed to notice its separate parts—contentedly oblivious to its components. When a film score suits a film perfectly, the soundtrack and picture seem inextricably connected. The marriage of film to original soundtrack is one of the last touches in a film's assembly.

Films begin silent. Just as the film's images evolve in distinct phases from individual pieces of celluloid to edited scenes to full-length picture–so the evolution of a film's music undergoes a similar metamorphosis.

We accept the marriage of film and music in a way that nearly defies explanation. With few exceptions, music in live theater is used sparingly–usually to bridge scenes, rarely to underscore the drama itself. (Musicals are an obvious exception.) Yet in movies, music is crucial.

Director Jonathan Kaplan (*Heart Like a Wheel*) says music "provides an emotional point of view, a theme, for the inner voice of the character that's much subtler than dialogue or imagery ... If it's good, it will provide the heart of the movie."

It is hard to determine exactly what makes a film score "good." Some scores are so subtle that one can hardly recall the music afterwards, and yet the film was enchanted by it. In other cases the viewer comes out humming the track. Film editor David Ray (*Death of a Salesman*) describes an original score as: "Music that comes out of nowhere... which helps to define the mood you're trying to achieve in the scene."

The first music a film experiences is neither written for the film nor original. This first phase of the score–the temp track or temp score–is intended to be a temporary stand-in for the music that will be composed later. Filmmakers often choose their temp tracks from their own classical, jazz, rock, Broadway musical, country western, or previous film score collections.

The director, film editor and composer have direct contact with the birth, life and death of the temp score. Although you rarely hear any of the temp score, your movie experience is affected by it.

At its best, the temp track can be a useful tool. It contributes to the editing process by helping editors to discover the "tone" or mood of a scene–what kind of music will help a scene play better. Editors experience the "rightness" or "wrongness" of particular music all the time. In fact, a standard exercise in film school is to view a scene with different music against it, thus enabling the viewer to actually play with different types of music.

Paul Hirsch (*Star Wars*), editor of the film *Obsession*, decided just for laughs to view a particular seduction scene with the music from *Psycho*'s shower scene; what was once romantic and sexy became diabolical.

Though the temp track can be useful in determining the "voice" of a picture, it should not necessarily be taken as the final word. Composer Miklos Rozsa (*Thief of Baghdad*) relates the story of his involvement on *The Lost Weekend*, a drama about alcoholism. The temp track of inappropriate gay, lively music prepared the audience for a comedy. After the first big laughs, the audience suddenly became confused and disgruntled upon discovering that the film was deadly serious. By the end of the sneak preview, hardly anyone remained in the theater. Rozsa was convinced that the sole problem with the picture was the misleading music. His more suitable original score complemented the dramatic elements of what became a successful film.

The editor may use a particular piece of music to inspire a good cutting sequence. Sometimes, in fact, the film will be cut exactly to the tempo of the music. This is called "Mickey Mousing," a term derived from the scoring of cartoons.

However, *Volunteers* editor Ronald Roose (*The Wanderers*) used Dimitri Tiomkin's pyramid building music from *Land of the Pharaohs* to create a particular rhythm. Later, composer James Horner (*Cocoon*) created an original score to match that established rhythm.

Very often the experimental period with the temp track will lead the filmmakers to a particular composer whose previous music they've discovered fits the film well.

Composers remain divided on the advisability of a temp track. Although composer Elmer Bernstein (*To Kill a Mockingbird*) is not a proponent of the temp track process, he admits that a temp track can help demystify the scoring process for the director: "Music is the most terrifying thing that happens to a director. A director speaks to a composer, tries to convey in literary terms what he wants but never knows what's going to happen until the music is actually being scored."

The temp score provides a common language for the director and composer. A composer is given a major hint of what the director is looking for by hearing what the director has used.

Aside from a handful of auteur directors, like Chaplin, who participated in the actual composing of the score, most filmmakers defer to the composer's expertise. However, many editors and directors admit that they experience a tremendous "rush" in the course of temp tracking their own films. In our luxurious video machine age a filmmaker can take home a copy of his film and screen it privately, going through his own records as he "test scores" his nearly completed work. Director Nicholas Meyer (*Time After Time*): "For a few glorious, insane, coincidental moments, you may make it work."

In the course of editing the film, scenes are added, subtracted, things are moved around. The film is shown countless times to audiences who are relatively fresh to the material. Temp track music is used also to cover the excess noise of the actual production track. This track contains the actors' dialogue as well as distracting, unintentional odd sounds–airplanes flying overhead, coughs, sneezes, general scratchiness. The temp track, according to editor Hirsch, is helpful at screenings since it "simulates the ultimate effect of how the picture will play, the finished product."

In the first of many screenings, the editor shows the director his first "assembly" of the picture. Director Jonathan Kaplan admits that music helps him when he sees the film for the first time. "Obviously I can't forget the movie, but I don't want to sit there and say, 'Boy, I think this is going to be exciting when there's music in it.'

The filmmakers feel additional strength in showing the unfinished film with a temp track on it to their financial backers. Director Jeremy Kagan (*Natty Gann*): "I like to show as finished a product as possible to those people so they have an idea what they're dealing with because they're not filmmakers. They are people, essentially audiences who have an enormous amount of power to say 'yes' or 'no.'"

Sometimes, the economic and time constraints do not allow the filmmakers the opportunity to fiddle with a temp track. Explaining the benefit of getting to temp track a film, editor David Ray describes what occurred on a particular project that was deprived of that opportunity: "It would have been very convenient to have had a temp track so we could try out things and live with them for a while. We had no time to experiment, so we made mistakes..."

Nowadays those mistakes are permanent or monstrously expensive to correct. In the old days when each studio had its own staff of writers, composers and an orchestra, a picture was scored and if it wasn't right, it was scored again. There were few budgetary and schedule considerations. Today if a film score doesn't meet with studio approval, it costs a fortune to record a new one. An equally pressing issue is time. The music is the last part of the film to be created before the final mix. It is often merely a matter of weeks before a film is released after it is scored. When a film score is thrown out, the entire postproduction schedule is thrown off kilter. Bookings in theaters must be rearranged. Total upheaval ensues.

Up until this point (during the assembly and first cuts of the film) the temp score has been useful. It has aided the editor and director in the editing process. It has assisted audiences and studio executives to imagine what kind of music will eventually exist.

There are, however, drawbacks to the use of a temp score. When you consider how many times a film is screened with its temp track, it is not surprising to find out that it can exert a powerful influence on the director, editor, composer, creative process and ultimately the final score. It is very difficult to dismiss the first musical association one has with a film. As composer James Horner said: "I need to know how long the temp track has been in the film. If it's been in for a long time, chances are people have grown very fond of it and will never be able to hear anything else."

It is for that very reason director Michael Pressman (*Some Kind of Hero*) doesn't like to add too much temporary music to his films. He likens the tremendous pull of the temp track over the original score with that of trying to hear another actor after having heard Lee J. Cobb do *Death of a Salesman*: "No matter how hard you try to separate yourself — it's there."

Pressman is aware of the danger of getting accustomed to the temp score. But what happens when the director unwittingly becomes addicted to it? There are two possibilities. The mere existence of a temp track may make it impossible for a director to imagine anything else in its place. The composer may be given clear instructions that a temp track works for the film and what is needed is a duplication just within the bounds of the law. This can be a sad situation for a creative composer who has to choose between disappointing the people who hired him by not fulfilling their preconceived ideas or earning himself a reputation as a "copier" because he tried to satisfy the demand.

A case in point. Stanley Kubrick hired Alex North (*Spartacus*) to write an original score for *2001*. When the picture opened, it contained none of North's music. Instead, it contained Richard Strauss' *Zarathustra*, Johann Strauss' *Blue Danube*, Gyorgy Ligeti as well as other familiar music. What happened? Kubrick fell in love with and remained faithful to his own temp track.

Composer Rozsa recalls working on a picture with a producer who loved the temp track. Every time an original Rozsa cue was played he would get angry and say: "It's not like the other one!" (The temp piece.) After hearing this numerous times Rozsa finally retorted: "No, of course it's not like the other one. I wrote it!" He finally quit.

Should a film not "work" in all its other elements prior to scoring, all hopes are pinned on the music to "save" the picture. To go with an unfamiliar yet original score takes confidence in the composer. The enormous pressure at this last stage of a film's creation begs for a "safe" bet... a temp track. Composer Bernard Herrmann, when called upon by Darryl Zanuck to rescue a film in deep trouble, wired: "I can dress the corpse, but I can't bring it to life."

Composer Rozsa had a curious experience when he worked with Alain Resnais on *Providence*. Upon hiring Rozsa, Resnais informed the composer that he would need 42 minutes of music. When Rozsa sat down to watch the film he was surprised to discover it was without the temp track. Clearly Resnais's use of a temp score had been for his own edification. He did not want to inhibit his composer's creativity.

Director Jonathan Kaplan is particularly sensitive to the merits of original music, perhaps in part because his father is composer Sol Kaplan (*The Spy Who Came in From the Cold*). Kaplan finds temp tracking helpful but prefers to use obscure music so it will not have an emotional association for those who hear it. "Music that is familiar can draw the viewer away from the picture. Instead of being caught up in the newly created world on the screen, the viewer wonders, 'Where have I heard this before?" says Kaplan.

The ideal way to temp track a film is to choose the composer early enough in the creation of the film for the composer himself to temp the film with the editor and director. This is done several ways. While working on *Max Dugan Returns*, director Herbert Ross (*Turning Point*) had composer David Shire (*All the President's Men*) play themes on a piano while screening scenes. This method, which has the composer acting as his own living temp track, allowed Ross to give Shire feedback right away, while at the same time giving Shire a clear image of what Ross was aiming for. Ross discovered this collaborative technique after enduring some painful scoring sessions in the past where he found the music to be wrong. Ross: "That day when the orchestra is sitting there is not the time to say to him, 'I knew you were wrong,' or 'Can you take out the strings?' You just have to suffer through that. It's too late for a conversation."

A final possibility is something composer Elmer Bernstein finds helpful. Most scoring sessions are done in consecutive days. Bernstein likes to spread the sessions out over a few weeks in order to get the director's response to the music with enough time to make changes. Bernstein maintains that filmmaking is a collaborative process. This system, he feels, allows the composer to fully participate while at the same time gives the director an opportunity for input on the music.

Ultimately, if the filmmakers are pressed for time, money or simply feel that the benefits of a temp track outweigh its drawbacks, then a temp score must be used thoughtfully so as not to undermine the contribution of the composer nor the film as a whole.

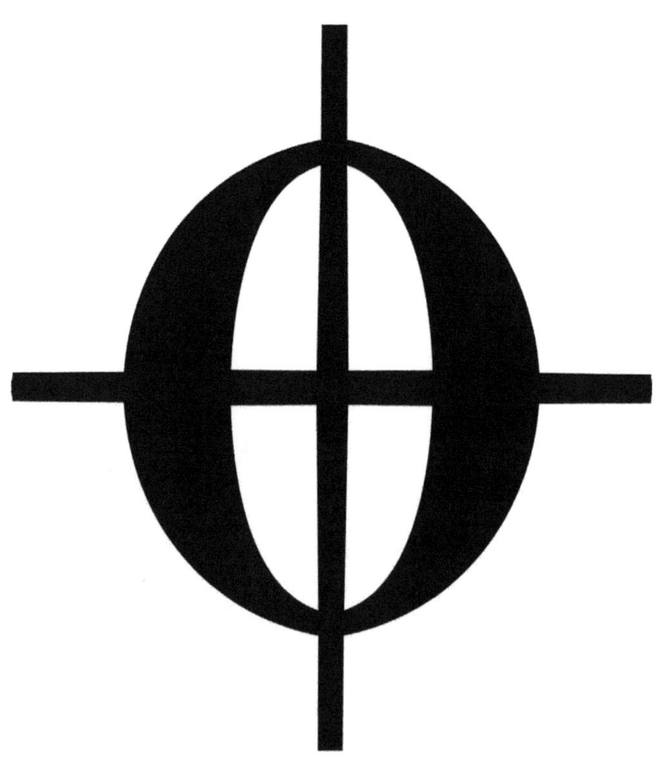

CODA

I loved getting to write these articles despite a few unpleasant repercussions.

In 1981 I was in the orchestra accompanying Kevin Brown-low's restored 1927 Abel Gance silent film *Napoleon.* Composer Carmine Coppola assembled the music for the 4-hour film. It was such an unusual experience to play that I wrote an article about it. Not knowing anyone at the Times, I sent my article [in] to the Calendar section. I received a letter from the desk of Irv Letofsky, the highly esteemed editor. It was a very thin envelope. I was certain that it was a rejection letter so I hadn't opened it. Weeks later, my brother called and asked whether I had heard back from the Times. I explained that the envelope was very thin so I hadn't opened it. Through gritted teeth, he said, "Do you still have it?" Shuffling through papers on my desk, I found it. "Getting an illustration done, will advise when it'll run −Irv". I nearly missed the publication date.

The film was a huge hit, so the run was extended. Twice. Shortly after the publication, and before the second rerun, the contractor called to let me know he had been instructed NOT to hire me again. Apparently, Coppola was furious that the article was not more about him. I asked the contractor whether it would help to send him the original eleven-page version that I had submitted to the LA Times, in which Coppola and his score was featured more prominently, but he said no. This was the beginning of an education about the vagaries of journalism, including the sensitive egos of composers and other artists.

I was at a concert the day my article on viola and violists came out. A number of colleagues were peeved with the illustration which featured a woman in a treble clef decorated dress, not the viola clef. I had nothing to do with the illustrations. I didn't see them until everyone did on Sunday morning when the paper came out.

But it was the Kirov article that caused me the greatest trouble. The Kirov Ballet run in Los Angeles was very big news. They hadn't been in LA in 22 years, following a spate of defections. I told the conductor in my very rusty Russian that I had written an article about him. Before leaving the pit for the first intermission of his last *Swan Lake* I handed the conductor a copy of the article (in English), and another copy to the dance critic, who was my contact at the Times. I was fired a few minutes later without explanation. Weeks later, I learned that the KGB had freaked out when they saw a member of the orchestra hand a white envelope to the Soviet conductor at his last performance. I had done it publicly, so no one would suspect me of anything nefarious. But they did anyway. A quick perusal of the article would have calmed the KGB down but no one bothered to read the article.

Professional musicians spend thousands of hours, usually starting in childhood, in solitary confinement honing their skills. It was fascinating for me to get to interview literally scores of musicians about things musical which I had no knowledge of. For the piece

about piano tuners, my 12-year-old daughter and I were thrilled
to meet Mr. Henry Steinway. Her enthusiasm was slightly reduced
when I said: "and he's so handsome!"

The resident accordionist with LA Opera groaned when I called
to ask if I could write an article about him.

"I want to understand what drew you to the instrument, and
what you love about it." Another groan.

"I'm a violinist as well as a writer," I added.

"Why didn't you say so in the first place! I'm so sick of being
interviewed by people who know nothing about music."

You take your chances when you wear more than one hat and
I certainly took mine. I don't regret having written any of these
articles. I loved talking to people about the specifics of their instrument and repertoire and was honored to call attention to these
Unsung Heroes.

CONSTANCE MEYER
Beverly Hills, California
December 1, 2025

ACKNOWLEDGEMENTS

This book would not have been possible without the cheering on of family, colleagues, and friends. I am grateful to several people: Craig Fisher, the former Deputy Editor of The Los Angeles Times Sunday Calendar section, who hired me in the first place, Adrienne Tripp, who insisted on building a website for me. Many thanks to Michael Singer, a childhood classmate who put the articles together in book form when I had no idea how to proceed. And much gratitude to Deniz Cordell who generously proof read my manuscript.

I am grateful to Theo Orion for his patience and lovely illustrations and to the remarkably gifted writer and guide Liz Dubelman, who showed me how to put one foot in front of the next in the self-publishing process.

A big thank you to my daughters, Natasha and Tatiana Spottiswoode, for encouraging me from the beginning and for being excellent proofreaders.

Many thanks to my brother, Nicholas, for pushing me to write and publish.

And finally, to my husband James, who urged me to start and keep going, and for doing everything he could possibly do to give me courage.

9 798995 384205